Yes, Your Butt STILL BELONGS IN CHURCH

ANSWERING THE EXCUSES THAT BLOCK MANKIND FROM HAVING LIFE AND HAVING IT MORE ABUNDANTLY

DANNY TYREE

Yes, Your Butt STILL BELONGS IN CHURCH

Answering the excuses that block mankind from having life and having it more abundantly

By: Danny Tyree

Yes, Your Butt STILL BELONGS IN CHURCH

Copyright ©2020 Danny Tyree

All rights Reserved

No part of this book may be used or reproduced in any manner whatsoever without written permission of the author.

Printed in the United States of America

ISBN: 979-8558182576

Author Publishing House
1801 Snake Creek Road
Belfast, TN 37019

Yes, Your Butt **STILL BELONGS IN CHURCH**

Table of Contents

Section 1

Getting Started **1**

    Dedication 2
    And a special thanks to Covid-19 3
    What seems to be the problem here? 5
    To whom is this book directed? 9
    Who am I and why do I feel compelled to write this book? 11
    The tone of this book 14

Section 2

The Excuses **17**

Excuse 1:	"Yeah, well, I gave up on Santa Claus a long time ago, too"	18
Excuse 2:	"But...lots of highly intelligent people reject Christianity"	25
Excuse 3:	"No, seriously, I don't need a crutch"	29
Excuse 4:	"There is too much suffering and evil in the world"	32
Excuse 5:	"God took my momma"	42

Yes, Your Butt STILL BELONGS IN CHURCH

Excuse 6:	"Church attendance is no guarantee of getting to heaven"	45
Excuse 7:	"Sunday is my one day a week to sleep in"	50
Excuse 8:	"The church is full of hypocrites"	54
Excuse 9:	"Church people have let me down"	58
Excuse 10:	"I don't want people knowing my business"	62
Excuse 11:	"I can read the Bible at home"	65
Excuse 12:	"Communing with nature does me just as much good as church"	69
Excuse 13:	"Meditation meets my spiritual needs"	74
Excuse 14:	"What I'm doing now is resonating with me just fine"	78
Excuse 15:	"I mean it: I'm happy with my alternatives"	82
Excuse 16:	"But I know what I'm doing"	89
Excuse 17:	"I'm a basically good person"	92
Excuse 18:	"But I shouldn't have to obey the rules"	95
Excuse 19:	"I'm too far gone to save"	98
Excuse 20:	"My family wasn't very religious"	103
Excuse 21:	"None of my friends go to church"	106
Excuse 22:	"My spouse/kids/ parents get enough religion for all of us"	110
Excuse 23:	"All they care about is your money"	114
Excuse 24:	"Church? That's not how I roll!"	117
Excuse 25:	"There's too much doctrine"	121
Excuse 26:	"Church is so boring"	125

Excuse 27:	"I'll wing it"	129
Excuse 28:	"My God wouldn't be such a hardnose"	132
Excuse 29:	"Church and my job don't mesh"	138
Excuse 30:	"God and I grew apart"	143
Excuse 31:	"I've got faith; I don't need works"	146
Excuse 32:	"If only I had a sign..."	150
Excuse 33:	"Hey, I send in my donations"	154
Excuse 34:	"Hey, I'm willing to settle"	156
Excuse 35:	"I've paid my dues"	160
Excuse 36:	"But what if..."	166
Excuse 37:	"I'm entitled to my loopholes"	170
Excuse 38:	"Okay, okay -- I'll get around to church eventually"	175

Section 3

All out of excuses; now what? *179*

What concerned Christians can do 180

What church leaders can do 184

What those outside the church can do 191

A final plea for apologetics 194

Why has this book taken so long? 198

Parting Words 207

Yes, Your Butt STILL BELONGS IN CHURCH

Section 1

Getting Started

Dedication

I don't have space to list all the people who have been important to my spiritual life (either by instructing me or challenging me to be a better example), but I would like to give a special nod to Ron Kleine (my minister for most of the past 50 years), his late wife Barbara, my parents (Margie Tyree and the late Lewis Tyree), my wife Melissa, and our son Gideon.

And a special thanks to Covid-19

Thank you, Covid-19 coronavirus, for letting me know I was on the right track.

I started writing this book several months before that pandemic turned the world upside down, but my experiences have hardened my resolve to get my message out to the public.

Based on the governor's recommendations, our church congregation suspended public worship services for five weeks. It was not a decision we took lightly; but many of our members are elderly or otherwise have compromised immune systems, and we didn't want their illness or deaths on our collective conscience.

Like many families, my wife, our teenage son, and I faithfully continued our Sunday worship services at home during the shutdown.

We prayed, sang hymns, read scripture, and discussed Bible lessons (sometimes from my wife's Ladies Class workbook, sometimes not). As baptized members, my wife and I partook of the Lord's Supper in remembrance of Christ's sacrifice for mankind.

This was a richly rewarding period of family togetherness, one I will always cherish. We could stumble over lyrics without making a public spectacle, get a point across with

Yes, Your Butt STILL BELONGS IN CHURCH

inside jokes that would be lost on other people, focus on issues specific to our family, etc.

But we were always aware that this was just a stopgap measure, an expedient, an "under the circumstances" substitute, a not-quite-satisfying workaround.

We have never felt the need to be lost in an auditorium filled with **thousands** of other congregants, but we knew that there was more to worship than just our intimate family circle.

We knew that we needed to see familiar faces, receive hugs and handshakes, be exposed to different perspectives, celebrate milestones (births, kindergarten graduations, retirements, etc.), offer a shoulder to cry on, and brainstorm the sort of ideas that show the church is greater than the sum of its parts.

The more we enjoyed our family bonding, the more we remained **vigilant** about the pitfalls of getting **too** comfortable, **too** cozy, **too** lazy with our cocoon-like worship services.

I set out several months ago to write a book about the continued relevance of communal public worship, of Christianity based on the Bible and not just "feel good" bumper stickers.

I never wavered in my dedication to the project, but Covid-19 did provide some extra "oomph" to see me over the finish line.

The Lord works in mysterious ways – but you must squeeze a few lemons to make the lemonade.

Yes, Your Butt STILL BELONGS IN CHURCH

What seems to be the problem here?

Have you ever worried that someday the account of the Empty Tomb might be preached to an Empty Auditorium?

If you're swaddled in the comfort of a vibrant megachurch, you may not realize how fragile the status of Christianity is.

But those of us in the trenches of more traditional churches (whether mainline or evangelical) can see Christ's influence becoming less and less relevant (to our daily lives, albeit not our eternal destination).

One of the main things that prevented this book from being finished sooner was that slogging through the myriad articles on the subject really took the wind out of my sails (if I may mix my metaphors). Studies/surveys were conducted in slightly different timeframes, with different terminology and different methodology. (For instance, the requirements for being a self-reported church "member" vary. And some studies lump all Jews, Christians, and Muslims together instead of focusing specifically on Christians.)

Rather than overwhelm you with page after page of conflicting statistics, I'll give you the gist of the trends, to buttress your own anecdotal accounts of what you've observed going on around you.

A Gallup News story from April 18, 2019 says that half of Americans belong to a church, synagogue, or mosque; that's **down from 70 percent** in 1999. Since the turn of the century, the percentage of U.S. adults with no religious

Yes, Your Butt STILL BELONGS IN CHURCH

affiliation has more than doubled, from 8 percent to 19 percent. Membership has dropped among all generational groups, contributing to the closing of thousands of U.S. churches each year. The authors of the report presumed that the nearly one-third of millennials without a religious preference are unlikely to ever join a church.

A Pew Research Center report released October 17, 2019 says that the number of religiously unaffiliated Americans (atheists, agnostics, "nothing in particular") now stands at 26 percent, up from 17 percent a mere decade earlier.

Even the sobering figures for decreased church membership can lead us into a false sense of security. Surveys tend to **set a low bar** for what it means to be a Christian.

You might think of a member as someone who is in the church building (eager and attentive) every Sunday morning come rain or shine (and who often attends on Sunday evening and Wednesday evening as well), someone who takes an active role in the church decision-making process, someone who is always ready to supply funding or elbow grease for church projects.

But surveys also count those who reply, "Um, yeah, we had our wedding at the Presbyterian church, so I guess I'm Presbyterian" or "My grandmother went to the Methodist church when she could, and I take after her side of the family more, so I guess you can put me down as Methodist."

According to Pew, more Americans now say they attend religious services **a few times a year or less** (54 percent) than say they attend **at least monthly** (45 percent). As I say, a low bar. Can you imagine bragging, "I show up for my assembly-line job at least monthly" or "I drag in to the school building to teach my third-graders at least three or four times a semester" or "Elm Street can sleep soundly because we conduct a Neighborhood Watch every time we get in the mood and there's nothing more interesting to do"?

The good news is that God, Christ, and the Holy Spirit are alive and well. The bad news is that **human respect** for the Trinity is swiftly eroding.

Why should it matter? A lot of people (both outsiders and church members) would be happy to see the stick-in-the-mud preacher have his pay frozen or watch the church keep patching together the same 30-year-old bus. But the decline of church membership, attendance, and donations also means less manpower and money for crisis pregnancy centers, grief counseling sessions, orphanages, food pantries, English as a Second Language courses, Third World medical missions, and the other good works performed by churches.

And what about the nation as a whole? People known as deists believe that God created the universe and then went far away, never ever intervening in the affairs of mankind again. My reading of the Bible does not jibe with that in the slightest. We have a history of God blessing the Jews (and their benefactors) when they are obedient and punishing them when they are disobedient. Secular history shows nations and empires being exalted and then – when they "get too big for their britches"—being thrown down.

I will not presume to micromanage God's responses to religious/irreligious behavior. I know some people declare without a moment's hesitation that "The Dow Jones Industrial Average soared 300 points because of a prayer offered up by Podunk Baptist Church last week" or "That tornado devastated Jackson Avenue because two or three years ago there was a gay pride parade four blocks over." I am trying to focus more on the **trending** impact of God on a nation's prosperity and security.

Yes, Your Butt STILL BELONGS IN CHURCH

If you believe in a Supreme Being at all, it is obvious that there is a **tipping point** when nations suffer either a slow decline or a calamitous downfall.

How near to the precipice is the United States? How far are we from getting on God's last nerve? No mere mortal knows. But lackadaisical church participation, the eroding of cultural norms, and the idolization of the most immoral among us do not paint an encouraging picture.

It gets worse. I've been writing about the Big Picture of governments and institutions and economies. But the most important impact of declining church influence is on the individual **souls** of human beings. As would-be congregants must drive farther and farther to find a church, as bright young adults become disinclined to view the ministry as a profession, as Bibles and church literature become less readily available, as church daycare centers become a scarcer venue for instilling a moral code, Satan finds limitless opportunities to tempt people onto a path that leads to hellfire.

So, the status of the church is vitally important on **multiple levels**.

Let's drop back to my first paragraph and whether you worry about the Empty Auditorium.

My wife and I have an ongoing, good-natured (I hope) disagreement about the definition of "worry." She flings the term about loosely, as in "Don't worry about fixing my coffee" or "Don't worry about mowing the lawn until later in the week." And I **don't** "worry" about the coffee or the lawn. In a very Yoda-like manner, I either do something or I don't do something. I reject defining "worry" to mean "go to a slight amount of trouble to accomplish something."

My definition of worry is "to be paralyzed by a pointless, sleep-disturbing wave of anxiety that seeks no resolution."

Yes, Your Butt **STILL BELONGS IN CHURCH**

So, when I inquire if you ever worry about the Empty Auditorium, I am not calling for a "woe is me" session of handwringing.

I am calling us to do some **problem-solving**.

And I humbly hope this book will play some small part in that problem-solving.

To whom is this book directed?

In a perfect world, this book would be snatched up by hundreds of millions of people from all walks of life and I would have oodles of money flowing into my retirement account and my church donations.

(Okay, technically, in a perfect world, there would be no **need** for this book. But I think you catch my drift.)

Considering that some people are more rigid about their spirituality than others, and factoring in my own intellectual limitations, I am taking the realistic approach and seeking a narrower readership.

If you are a dedicated lifelong adherent of Islam, Hinduism, Judaism, or some other established non-Christian religion, you are **not** the target of this book. Maybe someday I will write such a tome, but right now it is above my pay grade.

Nor is this book intended to change the worldview of someone who has come to their **atheism** through years of

Yes, Your Butt STILL BELONGS IN CHURCH

contemplation. (In the late 80s and early 90s, when I was a columnist for **Comics Buyer's Guide** magazine, I briefly corresponded with prolific author Harlan Ellison – perhaps best known to the general public for scripting the "City on the Edge of Forever" episode of the original *Star Trek*. Ellison had always been outspoken about a lot of things, including his atheism. Fast forward to late June of 2018. Although I had written to Ellison only once in the past 35 years, I suddenly had the notion that I might be the person perfectly positioned to create some cracks in his skepticism. I started juggling some ideas to send in his direction. Within two or three days, I received news of his death. Now, I'm not saying God took Ellison at that time to teach me a lesson in humility, but it makes you wonder.)

No, I'm directing this book at four specific groups.

If you used to attend church (as a full-fledged member or tagging along with your family) but either gradually drifted away or abruptly quit in anger or disillusionment, this book is for you.

If you are currently occupying a pew but are counting the days until you can quit or scale back your participation, this book is for you.

If your family has never really been church-going, but you are Christian-adjacent and would be open to learning more, this book is for you.

If you are a person of unwavering faith who intends to gather with God's people until you are no longer physically able -- but you are concerned about the national surveys or the familiar faces you no longer see across the aisle – this book is for you.

If I can be of some measure of help to those of you in the first three categories, I hope you will recommend this volume to your friends.

If those of you in the fourth category see merit in my reasoning/presentation, I encourage you to buy an extra copy to put in the church library. Or maybe you could buy multiple copies to pass out to members, visitors, and strangers.

It won't make **this** a perfect world, but it might prepare a few more folks for a realm that **is** perfect.

Who am I and why do I feel compelled to write this book?

I have attended the same rural church since I was a few weeks old.

This is the same congregation where my mother had been baptized 13 years earlier, where I would be baptized at age 15, and where my father would serve as an elder up until the time of his death.

When my wife and I got married (1991), we toyed with the idea of making a fresh start with a different congregation, but she was made to feel so welcome that we stuck with my heritage.

This is the church where I have been in the rotation to teach an adult Bible class for more than 35 years. It is the church where I have been a deacon for the past several years.

Yes, Your Butt STILL BELONGS IN CHURCH

During my six decades at this congregation, I have seen all sorts of scenarios. I've seen four generations of congregants sharing a pew. I've seen new families move in and invite their friends. I've seen members depart in anger because of a personal conflict with another member. I've seen kids grow up, get out from under their parents' roof, and never darken the doors of the church again. I've seen kids grow up, get married, and raise a Christian family in another congregation. I've seen unchurched people coming to church late in their lives.

Between my experiences in my home congregation, observing other congregations in the community, and being a lifelong news junkie (keeping up with trends such as those mentioned in the introduction), I feel I have the foundation for committing my observations to paper.

I often wrote about moral issues for my college newspaper – Middle Tennessee State University's *Sidelines*. (After I wrote a pro-life article, a valiant anonymous classmate left a "Your mother should have aborted **you**" note in my locker.) When I was writing for *Comics Buyer's Guide*, I was infamous for an essay titled "Why Doesn't Batman Go to Church?" Most of my weekly newspaper columns (syndicated internationally by Cagle Cartoons) are humorous, but I try to weave in a few somber essays, especially near Easter and Christmas.

Okay, but why commit to writing an entire book? And why now?

Well, I have a lot of love and concern for my fellow man, but there is also the factor of **self-preservation**.

Writing is one of the few things I do well. I am not a handyman, a woodworker, a glassblower, a shade-tree mechanic, a computer hacker, or a basketball wizard.

Yes, Your Butt STILL BELONGS IN CHURCH

I am good at organizing my thoughts, stringing words together, and polishing my message. I've employed that in writing my columns, delivering speeches, and writing commercials for my day-job employer.

My writing has evolved through mentoring, constructive criticism, and inspiration, but at its core it remains a **God-given talent**.

And God **expects** us to use our God-given talents.

I dread facing a **Judgment Day** in which I haven't used my God-given talents.

I don't think God will erase my name from the Book of Life just because I've given readers a smile over naked vacations, facial tattoos, feline-friendly motels, and other trivia.

I **do** think He will have misgivings about my worthiness if I have **solely** focused on silly, ephemeral things (in other words, not fully utilized the talent He bestowed upon me).

So, for the sake of my own eternal reward, I am eager to prioritize getting this book out to the public.

And because of the conditions mentioned in the introduction, I want to get it out there before another church closes or another member drifts away.

The Tone of this Book

Most of the rest of this book will be short chapters spotlighting different reasons (excuses) that people use for dropping out of church, participating only minimally in church, or never giving Christianity a chance in the first place.

I write with love in my heart. I write out of concern for fellow humans. I try not to be condescending, since I am a fallible human myself.

But some of the excuses are so illogical, so irrational, so trite, so self-destructive, so **exasperating** that I may be tempted to shake someone by the collar and shout, "What part of this do you not understand, you chowderhead???"

I'll try to be civil, diplomatic, compassionate, and understanding. As has often been pointed out in our adult Bible classes, "You don't draw someone nearer to Christ by jumping on them with both feet."

I have not written a book about bad **people**.

I have written a book about **bad behavior** and **faulty reasoning**.

Defensive people will splutter, "You're lying! You're a hater! It's not possible to love the sinner but hate the sin!"

I'm not sure what makes these people think they can read my mind or the minds of millions of other Christians ("I don't know what number you're thinking of or the name of your first pet or your favorite flavor of ice cream, but I

know you're an intolerant ogre – you just have to be!"), but I know that I'm trying my best to write an accessible call to repentance.

I hope you'll respect me for not sanitizing my message and pulling my punches.

Yes, Your Butt STILL BELONGS IN CHURCH

Section 2

The Excuses

Excuse 1:

"Yeah, well, I gave up on Santa Claus a long time ago, too"

I originally planned to start off with a different excuse, but this one is just so fundamental that I switched gears.

I mean, **if** God doesn't exist and Jesus didn't die for our sins and the Bible has been distorted beyond recognition over the centuries...Christian (and all monotheistic worship) is based on a lie. It doesn't **matter** if the other excuses are lame or illogical. You don't **need** any of the other excuses **if** this one is valid.

It's like if you're **not married**, it's pointless to obsess over concocting excuses to give your **non-existent spouse** when you stagger into the house at 3 a.m. (On the other hand, if you **are** married, your explanations had better be able to withstand intense scrutiny.)

I believe with all my heart that the snarky comment about Santa Claus is just a **false equivalency**.

False equivalencies **abound** in our modern world.

Yes, Your Butt STILL BELONGS IN CHURCH

We have lost any sense of proportionality and discernment. Exaggeration, hyperbole, oversimplification, and fearmongering are the order of the day with emotional, hair-trigger citizens.

Every politician you disagree with is **exactly** like Hitler, and every policy that miffs you is **exactly** like the Holocaust.

The slightest curtailment of something you've been getting away with is **exactly** like Mussolini's fascist regime.

If someone questions the motives and tactics of an organization you belong to, it's **exactly** like a revival of the Salem witch trials or McCarthyism.

If someone tries to stem the tide of illegal immigrants seeking free stuff from the U.S. government, it's **exactly** the same as turning away Jews who were fleeing for their lives from Hitler.

Any police interaction with minorities or any fine-tuning of entitlements is **exactly** the same as Jim Crow laws, "separate but unequal" facilities, and lynching.

Parents setting a curfew or expecting reimbursement for gasoline is **exactly** like slavery.

Getting an abortion is **exactly** like getting a mammogram.

And in our increasingly secular world, it's just a "given" that Jesus Christ is **exactly** the same as Santa Claus, the Easter Bunny, the Tooth Fairy, a mythological sun god riding his chariot across the sky, the earth resting on the back of a giant turtle, etc.

Yes, the Savior is treated to be just as real and plausible (no more, no less) than all the fairy tales, legends, myths, superstitions, and old wives' tales that have accumulated over the course of human history.

Yes, Your Butt STILL BELONGS IN CHURCH

Of course, this is seen as a godsend (no pun intended) for those who seek loopholes to ease their burden of guilt, time constraints, and obligations. It's a windfall, a "get out of jail free" card.

"If there is no God and no Jesus, then all the Sunday mornings for the rest of my life have opened up. And I can redirect that donation money to a new boat. And I can go back to hating my jerk of a next-door neighbor. And I can renew my membership at the STDs R Us Gentlemen's Club..."

Not to rain on anyone's pleasure parade, but if you're honest with yourself, Jesus Christ is **infinitely** more grounded in reality than monsters hiding under the bed or fairies dancing on the lawn.

Yes, the invocation of Santa's name can persuade children to refrain from punching their siblings for a couple of months, but does any intelligent adult have second thoughts about substance abuse, adultery, or cannibalism because of Kris Kringle?

Soldiers willingly risk their lives (just as the early Christians and the strongest of today's Christians face martyrdom), but it is for **real people** (their families and neighbors) rather than for an abstract "Uncle Sam."

Has anyone ever prayed to the Tooth Fairy and received a miraculous cure or the opening of a window of opportunity – or it is just five bucks under the pillow?

Sure, the North American Aerospace Defense Command (NORAD) plays along and has a tongue-in-cheek Santa Tracker keeping up with the progress of Santa and his sleigh every Christmas Eve, but have there **ever** been any serious, sober news accounts of Santa Claus?

Did the first "appearance" of the Easter Bunny **fulfill** any prophecies?

Yes, Your Butt STILL BELONGS IN CHURCH

Did a Yeti or a leprechaun or Zeus ever **make** any prophecies that came true?

Is the typical myth rooted in **specific times and places**, or is it more "once upon a time in a wonderful land"?

Have archaeologists ever verified anything about Santa's workshop at the North Pole?

Of course, the answer to these rhetorical questions is "No." On the other hand, there is no shortage of **corroborating evidence** for the existence and divinity of Jesus Christ.

Christians are constantly derided as being "narrow-minded," but blithely dismissing the Savior as just a campfire story is the epitome of narrow-mindedness.

It grieves me that millions of people have been blinded to this all-important fact. However they arrive at this point in life, it is a tragic situation.

Perhaps God chose not to cure their 99-year-old grandmother of stage-4 cancer. Perhaps they became infatuated with a "free-thinking" new boyfriend or girlfriend who asked questions their parents couldn't answer. Perhaps an atheistic college professor made an all-out assault on their beliefs. Maybe they came in halfway through one of those sensationalized History Channel documentaries that claims Jesus was quintuplets and that the Dead Sea Scrolls were actually written…last Tuesday afternoon.

People with these life experiences wind up on various points on the skepticism spectrum. Some are thoroughly convinced that God, Jesus, heaven, and hell are all fake. Some have "souped-up" agnosticism and bounce back and forth constantly. Some have a half-hearted attitude that permits the other excuses to gain a foothold.

Satan can use any of these positions on the spectrum to serve his purposes. But it doesn't have to be that way.

Yes, after the last of the eyewitnesses of Christ died...after the last of the early Christians who were given a special portion of the Holy Spirit passed away...mankind was faced with centuries of being given a "take it or leave it" ultimatum by priests or circuit-riding preachers.

But we now live in a Golden Age of biblical **apologetics** – a branch of theology that advances and defends the Bible against objections.

I'm sure you've heard (or used) the most common objections – some of them wildly contradictory. "Jesus never even existed." "Jesus was just a good man who grew to Paul Bunyan status over the centuries." "Jesus – the good man who never existed – faked his own death." "The church suppressed other gospels that were 100 percent as valid as Matthew, Mark, Luke and John." "Either accidentally or on purpose, all the key doctrines of the original New Testament have been corrupted over time." "The Bible is full of contradictions." "Science has proven there is no need for God or His Son."

Like "doubting Thomas" being invited to touch the wounds of Christ, we are invited to explore things that might dispel our unbelief.

The Case for Christ: A Journalist's Personal Investigation of the Evidence for Jesus and companion books by Lee Strobel are possibly the most **famous** apologetics books, but they are just the tip of the iceberg.

At the end of this chapter, I have listed several other apologetics books. Some of these I have read more than once. Some I have speed-read. Some are written from a scholarly perspective (with ten-dollar words such as "hermeneutics"). Some are written for the average person.

Yes, Your Butt STILL BELONGS IN CHURCH

Some are omnibus editions answering multiple objections. Some zero in on a particular issue. But all are useful for making it possible to be **confident about Christian faith**. And – as of this writing – all are conveniently available on Amazon.

I am not going to force anyone to read these books, but whether you are an unbeliever or a Christian who is constantly bombarded with questions you can't answer, these books have immeasurable value.

Just remember that **willful ignorance** comes with consequences.

If you violate a major appliance's warranty because you couldn't be bothered to read the owner's manual, you suffer the consequences.

If you arrogantly walk into a job interview cold, without brushing up on the company's background, you suffer the consequences.

If you break a company policy because it was too much trouble to read a prime protocol on **page one of the employee handbook**, you suffer the consequences.

If scholars painstakingly explain reasons for believing the Gospel and you are too busy or too **whatever** to avail yourself of those resources, you suffer the consequences.

Don't back yourself into a corner by **making excuses for making excuses**.

If you're prideful enough to scoff, "I don't need no stinkin' apologetics books," that's proof that you **do** desperately need them. As Proverbs 16:18 tells us, "Pride goes before destruction, and a haughty spirit before a fall."

Glance at the list. Remember where you found it. Then we can move on to the next excuse.

Yes, Your Butt STILL BELONGS IN CHURCH

- *Answering the Toughest Questions About Suffering and Evil*, by Bruce Bickel and Stan Jantz
- *Can We Trust the Gospels?: Investigating the Reliability of Matthew, Mark, Luke, and John*, by Mark D. Roberts
- *Darwin Devolves: The New Science About DNA That Challenges Evolution*, by Mike Behe
- *Faith on Trial: Analyze the Evidence for the Death and Resurrection of Jesus*, by Pamela Binnings Ewen
- *Answers to Common Questions About the Bible*, by H. Wayne House and Timothy J. Demy
- *Answers to Common Questions About God*, by H. Wayne House and Timothy J. Demy
- *Answers to Common Questions About Jesus*, by H. Wayne House and Timothy J. Demy
- *Gospel Powered Apologetics: How to Defend A Reasonable Faith*, by Sterling Carroll
- *The Historical Reliability of the Gospels*, by Craig L. Blomberg
- *The Politically Incorrect Guide to Darwinism and Intelligent Design*, by Jonathan Wells
- *The Emmaus Code: Finding Jesus in the Old Testament*, by David Limbaugh
- *Jesus Is Risen: Paul and the Early Church*, by David Limbaugh
- *The Historical Jesus: Ancient Evidence for the Life of Christ*, by Gary Habermas
- *The Case for the Resurrection of Jesus*, by Gary R. Habermas and Michael Licona

Excuse 2:

"But...lots of highly intelligent people reject Christianity"

Assuming a standard definition for "highly intelligent" (high I.Q., high Grade Point Average, stacks of academic degrees, gets labeled as an "expert" on CNN or Fox News), yes, a lot of highly intelligent people do stay away from church.

(Conversely, a lot of highly intelligent people today and in ages past **have** been strong Christians. But let's ignore that for the moment.)

Don't fool yourself into thinking that all intelligent people are in lockstep, sharing a single mind. Activists like to throw around the word "consensus," but I'll bet you can't think of a single thing that intelligent people **unanimously** endorse.

Check it out. You'll find highly intelligent people disagreeing vehemently over the best way for the Federal Reserve Board to control inflation, the number of troops to

Yes, Your Butt STILL BELONGS IN CHURCH

maintain in Afghanistan, how to conquer Covid-19, whether the models for predicting the effects of climate change are remotely accurate, the best way to reduce crime, and countless other topics.

Highly intelligent people might differ by **billions of years** on their estimation of the age of the universe. (Let's hope they keep getting their astrophysics grants; they probably wouldn't make much working the "Guess your age and weight" booth at the carnival.)

So even if you have a "follow the crowd" or "there's safety in numbers" philosophy of life, there's no guarantee that you'll follow the **right** segment of highly intelligent people on issues of geopolitics, physics, engineering, religion, or whatever.

People who are highly intelligent are rarely highly intelligent about **everything**. We celebrate the notion of a "Renaissance man" who excels in everything he does, but put those people under a microscope and they will eventually be found wanting.

Someone may be a math whiz but be totally clueless that one of their co-workers is in love with them. Someone may be able to sketch out a cutting-edge bridge on a paper napkin but be unable to operate a stick-shift to **drive over** that bridge when it's constructed. Someone may be able to compose brilliant symphonies in their head but be **tone-deaf** as to the ways they hurt the feelings of those around them.

Surely, you've heard or experienced skepticism over "book learnin'" when you were growing up. Rightly or wrongly, I've often heard people with "book smarts" described derisively as not having enough common sense to pour (urine) out of a boot.

Yes, Your Butt STILL BELONGS IN CHURCH

Even highly intelligent people make mistakes. Journalist David Halberstam's 1972 book *The Best and the Brightest* (published by Random House) shows how the **academics and intellectuals** who were in Pres. John F. Kennedy's administration formulated foreign policy that got us into the quagmire of the Vietnam War.

Society seems to go to extremes on its treatment of intelligent people. We either resent them or place them on a pedestal. But many have feet of clay. They may be geniuses at biochemistry or mystery-novel writing or skyscraper-building, but it's likely they eat the wrong foods or get too little sleep or trust crooked investment coaches or forget to floss or hang out with fair-weather friends or **something**. Jesus Christ is the only **perfect** person who has ever walked the earth.

Sometimes highly intelligent people just don't **use** the intelligence that they've been given. Christians generally regard King Solomon as the wisest human who ever lived (if you don't count Jesus), but it's as if he sometimes chose to flip the "off" switch on his intelligence when it suited him. Some combination of physical lust, greed and political ambition caused him to collect foreign wives and concubines. Solomon's acceptance of their pagan worship started all sorts of hardship for him and his posterity.

If you admire someone for their preeminence in a particular field, feel free to check out their feelings on spirituality. But take those beliefs with a grain of salt.

People of all intelligence levels arrive at their religious viewpoint through numerous factors. Focusing on people who choose **not** to participate in traditional worship, let's consider the possible factors. Maybe their parents didn't set a good example. Maybe they were brainwashed by a teacher or another authority figure. Maybe they are just too prideful to admit the existence of a Higher Power. Maybe they are fearful of being ostracized by their peers. Maybe

Yes, Your Butt STILL BELONGS IN CHURCH

they just like having Sunday as their fun day (their "I don't have to run day," as the Bangles sang.)

In short, don't automatically **assume** that a highly intelligent person skips church membership or church attendance solely because they **purged their preconceptions** and **applied 110 percent of their analytical skills** to figuring out the right spiritual path, any more than they purge their preconceptions and apply 110 percent of their analytical skills when channel surfing on a Friday night or grabbing a bag of potato chips on a quick trip to the convenience market.

Cling to "Lots of highly intelligent people don't go to church" if you must, but in fact it's about as relevant as "Lots of skinny people or lots of blonde people or lots of left-handed people or lots of people with peanut allergies or lots of 42-year-old suburban people don't go to church."

Excuse 3:

"No, seriously, I don't need a crutch"

In the 1840s philosopher Karl Marx wrote the German words that are commonly translated as "religion...is the opiate of the masses."

After nearly two centuries those who have "outgrown" God or never embraced God in the first place still hold that prejudice.

To them, religious people are a vast ocean of contemptible, interchangeable, illiterate serfs who need a crutch or a drug to endure life.

If you're honest with yourself, you'll recognize that it is impossible to put such a one-size-fits-all label on believers.

Shifting our focus to Christians in particular, since the beginning of the church, worshippers have included a broad cross-section of humanity: different ages, nationalities, income levels, occupations, etc.

Yes, Your Butt STILL BELONGS IN CHURCH

Look at the church membership in any good-sized town or city. Yes, you'll find people who had to drop out of high school to support their families, widows who never worked outside of the home, and citizens who have never traveled more than a hundred miles from home. (Not that there's anything wrong with any of these situations.)

There are also doctors, lawyers, mayors, world-traveling business executives, college professors, journalists, and others whom we would recognize as confident, educated, successful members of society.

Sure, some of them are opportunists who use church mostly for networking; but most are sincere, stable, contributing pillars of the community.

Most of them have the education, the people skills, the confidence, and the financial resources to **muddle through** the vagaries of life on their own **reasonably** well; but they want to **have life and have it more abundantly**.

They have the intelligence and the humility to realize that there is more to existence than their credentials or their bank account.

They understand that someday **every** knee will bow before Christ, but right now they are not groveling or submitting to brainwashing. They enjoy a **respectful friendship** with Christ. They are using the knowledge God has given them to be better people and prepare for their eternal home.

It is intellectually dishonest to pretend that only religious people need a crutch or an "opiate." With all the IRS audits, natural disasters, back-stabbings, layoffs, and untimely deaths that the world throws at us, **everyone** needs **something** to stay sane and functioning.

Yes, Your Butt STILL BELONGS IN CHURCH

It might be sexual conquests, bodybuilding, status symbols, political power, packrat tendencies, or some other distraction; but everyone needs **some way** to hold their heads up and persevere.

It is shortsighted for the irreligious to look down their noses on the folks who find meaning, comfort, and guidance in the teachings of Christ.

Those other support systems do not necessarily make the world a better place or prepare you for the next world.

Those sixpack abs will not transcend the physical world. Even worldly people understand the "You can't take it with you" attributes of earthly wealth. Building a bigger garage to house your latest antique-car acquisition might put some more money in the contractor's pocket, but you get no credit for doing it out of the kindness of your heart. You might grudgingly share your vape cartridge or your heroin needle with someone else, but you are not really giving them **hope**.

Mature Christians are **not** clinging to a security blanket or a pacifier; they have found the answers to life's biggest questions and are trying to spread the Good News, voluntarily helping other people with their burdens.

Karl Marx's legacy? It is one of class envy, authoritarian rule, thought control, murder, and economic stagnation.

Whose example would you prefer to follow?

Yes, Your Butt STILL BELONGS IN CHURCH

Excuse 4:
"There is too much suffering and evil in the world"

"Why is there so much suffering and evil in the world?" is a legitimate question – up to a point.

It seems to be one of the Three Big Questions for mankind, along with "Why am I here?" and "Is there anything after this life?"

Unfortunately, people tend to be egocentric with their questions. These "woke" individuals think they are the **first person in history** who has recognized such conundrums.

I have stumbled across umpteen references that essentially say, "Mankind has wrestled with these questions for millennia."

Indeed, hundreds of books and millions of sermons have dealt with the existence of suffering and evil in the world.

Perhaps I'm spoiled and have led a sheltered existence, but I've never really had to **wrestle** with the questions. I may have started the grieving process with "Why wouldn't that girl grant me a second date?" or "Why did someone else win the promotion I wanted?" or "Why did a speeding car happen to be coming along at exactly the time my cat was crossing the road?" – but I always cycle on through the stages of grief.

I'm not bragging, but I have enough maturity and spiritual grounding to ask "Why?" – and then **get on with my life**.

But some people are inconsolable. They exhibit anger, disillusionment, and despair no matter how articulately or frequently someone answers their question.

For them, the fact that God doesn't act exactly the way they want is prima facie evidence that (a) He doesn't exist or (b) He is not powerful enough or loving enough to deserve their respect. They drown their sorrows by drinking, beating their spouse/children, or accumulating "stuff."

When I first decided to write a spirituality book, it was going to be **focused** on the evil/suffering issue. I ultimately decided to concentrate on church attendance. I may eventually **write** that book centered on evil and suffering, but for now I would like to do a condensed message in this chapter.

My comments may elicit a stream of "But...but...but..."; but please hear me out.

God created a good world and placed man in charge of it. God created man in His own image. Some take this as proof positive that God has two eyes, ten fingers, ten toes, and all the attributes we connect with a healthy specimen of homo sapiens; more serious scholars think the main point is that we are **free moral agents** with the ability to make choices – and suffer the everlasting **consequences** of those choices.

Satan (in the form of a serpent) entered the Garden of Eden and deceived Eve; Adam went along with his wife.

Yes, Your Butt STILL BELONGS IN CHURCH

Mankind fell from grace with God. Sin, death, and decay entered the world.

Yes, pain, discomfort, hard work, illness, aging, and eventually returning to dust all came as part of that sin.

Each person since Adam and Eve has contributed to the problem in his own way – sometimes with small sins and sometimes in flamboyant cruelties such as the actions of the Roman emperors.

God sent His only begotten Son to die for our sins and give us hope of eternal life (as well as to set an example for us of how to lighten the burden of our fellow man during our time on earth).

That's it in a nutshell. I have been given no reason to doubt the veracity or the comprehensiveness of this answer.

You may splutter and harumph and conjure up extraneous sub-questions, but that's on **you**.

In 1979 comedian Robin Williams released an album titled *reality...what a concept*. We would do well to remember what a **stubborn thing** reality is. You might close your eyes, plug your ears, and curl into a fetal position because your sister is dating a hoodlum, the city council doubled the property tax, or the screenwriter of a movie sequel ruined one of the characters; but your caterwauling and denial does not change the fact that these unpleasant things actually took place.

And your protestations do not change the fact that God has provided us with a reasonable explanation of why death, suffering, and evil exist.

God's ways are not our ways, but we are slow to admit that we operate from a **limited frame of reference.**

Even the most trusting pet becomes anxious when hauled in a pet porter and jabbed with a big needle (for their own

Yes, Your Butt STILL BELONGS IN CHURCH

good) by a veterinarian. Low-level employees (not privy to the accounting ledgers) "know" that upper management is holding out on them and that the CEO should magically give everyone a $5-an-hour raise and six weeks of vacation (even though the bottom line shows that the business is on the brink of bankruptcy). My little brother and I thought our mother was being mean and unreasonable when she wouldn't let us spend the dimes Granny Tyree gave us while she was dying of cancer in Leonard's Hospital; but now I'm glad I still have my dime as a keepsake.

We are terrible judges of time and healing. We carry a child's "This is the worst day of my life!" attitude with us. True, some people carry a scar or a limp forever, but **most** of our crises become mere memories.

Intellectually, I know that I had all the common childhood diseases (including a near-fatal case of whooping cough), that I broke my arm at age seven, that I got dumped by my first girlfriend, that I broke my ankle at age 30, that I totaled a car soon after getting married, that I spent seven months unemployed after being downsized, that I suffered excruciating pain before prostate surgery, etc.

I might shudder and reminisce about lost opportunities, but I do not experience phantom pain or suffer PTSD flashbacks. A lot of these life experiences are things I can laugh about now.

"Time heals all wounds" is a simplistic motto, but it's not exactly **wrong**. It doesn't work the same for all people in all circumstances, but it does tend to put things in perspective.

I'm not yearning to wreck **another** car, but I've had enough offsetting joys over the years and enough new challenges every day that I don't **dwell** on such mishaps.

Yes, Your Butt STILL BELONGS IN CHURCH

Misfortune can be a learning experience. We can learn patience, empathy, priorities, how to help others, how to recognize silver linings.

But sometimes we must be dragged kicking and screaming into it.

Too often adults act like petulant children, with a Whac-A-Mole cascade of "Why? Why? Why? Why?" questions.

You know what I'm talking about with childhood questions: "Why **can't** I just go straight to high school from nursery school?" "Why **can't** I live on nothing but macaroni and cheese?" "Why **won't** you and momma make me a twin brother?"

We want God to fix everything on **our** terms. It's the old "Well, if **I** were God, I would …" mindset. That's an old mindset and a **naive** mindset. Believe it or not, I think most presidential candidates do make some sincere promises. But when they face the opposition party, the other branches of government, an entrenched bureaucracy, and a hostile press, they are shocked to find they cannot deliver half the things they "knew" they could produce. Multiply that a bazillion times to see how puny our understanding of God's job is.

We experience our own setbacks and see video of Eastern European refugees and decide that God had darned well better do something – **anything** – to alleviate the problem.

Do people even know what they are asking? How would it work?

Follow with me: we currently have mortal bodies, physical laws, limited natural resources, freedom-loving personalities, and conflicting goals.

Yes, Your Butt STILL BELONGS IN CHURCH

A lot of our physical/emotional/financial pain comes from naturally occurring **competition**. I can't fathom how we can have people competing for the same pool of mates, jobs, honors, houses, etc. **without** there being winners and losers. It would be a bigger miracle than calming the sea or feeding 5,000 people with five loaves and two fishes **if** you could guarantee that 100 percent of the people would be 100 percent happy 100 percent of the time, given our present restrictions.

As long as we're living on planet Earth, there is a constant need for food, clothing, shelter, and **sense of purpose**. God could rein in the natural disasters (lightning strikes, earthquakes, etc.) and make us physically and morally perfect, incapable of making careless mistakes or shoddy products; but what would become of all the doctors, nurses, lawyers, policemen, firemen, scrap collectors, crime novelists, crime reporters, undertakers, dent-removing body shop employees…? The list goes on and on. The people with those skills and interests would have no income, no contribution to make, no reason to get up in the morning.

We complain about the inevitability of physical death, but we don't want to ponder the implications of its **absence**. We think it would be cool to chat with Socrates, Thomas Jefferson, Mozart, Charles Darwin, or Napoleon; but if we're going to be fair about it, God couldn't grant immortality to just a **handful of elites**.

No, the earth would be populated with hundreds of generations of people, from Adam on down. The people killed by the Flood, the Philistines, the Babylonians, the Visigoths, the Huns, the Mayans, the Aztecs, the Incans, the Mongols, the Vikings, and countless other humans would all be crowded together, trying to get their share of the same limited resources.

Yes, Your Butt STILL BELONGS IN CHURCH

We already complain about overpopulation, pollution, urban sprawl, high-rises that blot out the sun, hunger, and carbon footprints; but what else could you expect in a world where God capitulated to shortsighted human demands and let everyone live forever?

Don't think that your life would be exactly the same (only better!) if God rebooted the earth in the way some people imagine. If you obtained your job because Mr. Jones got old and frail and had to retire, or if you were able to buy your current home because Mrs. Smith died and the house was put on the market, your life would be drastically changed. You might not even **be** here. If this overcrowding had been going on for thousands of years, surely at some point someone would have tried curtailing the birth rate (either voluntarily or under compulsion). Maybe your great-great-great grandparents would never have been born – meaning no **you**, either!

Until we live in a spiritual realm, it's not enough just to have physical health and immortality. There would always be humans who are not "team players": bullies, tyrants, abusers, bigots. swindlers.

"Oh, God could **make** us be good," you might blurt out.

But how many people seriously want to give up **free will**? ("Well, **those** people should have their free will removed, but of course I get to **keep** mine.") How many of us want to be God's preprogrammed **robots**? Countless science fiction and super-hero stories have dealt with megalomaniacs who try to rewire the thought patterns of the entire world's population. No matter how well-meaning these characters are, we invariably view them as **villains**.

"Well, God could let us retain our free will, but He could be more proactive about stopping us from **abusing** our free will," you might counter.

That sounds pretty good, but sin is sin. In all fairness, you couldn't limit your definition to just rape, armed robbery, and genocide. There are innumerable lesser infractions that a pure, just, holy God would be obligated to stop dead in their tracks.

And remember, God judges our **thoughts** as well as our actions.

God is not the author of confusion (1 Corinthians 14:33), but Earth would be in complete chaos as angels (either visible or invisible) zoomed around, smashing into each other while they went about smiting, tripping, zapping, slapping humans to keep them from breaking God's laws.

Someone would get a punch in the nose, a pinch, a kick in the rump, or a shock-collar effect every time they teased another person, told a white lie, misappropriated a handicapped parking spot, oozed through a red traffic light, parked in the fire lane for "just a minute," kept the too-generous change that a clerk handed them by mistake, stole office supplies, laughed at a dirty joke, used up the roll of toilet paper without replacing it, or undressed a pedestrian with their eyes.

All of this might be hilarious to you – until it is **your** sins that get preemptively addressed.

The peace of God, "which passeth all understanding" (1 Timothy 4:6) keeps the hearts and minds of Christians through Christ Jesus; but there would be no peace in the "utopia" envisioned by people who demand that God make the present earth perfect.

People sometimes make an off-color remark and then jokingly glance to make sure God doesn't hit them with a bolt of lightning. But that would be a serious, constant reality in man's "utopia." Every minute of every day we would be on edge as we waited for the other shoe to drop.

Yes, Your Butt STILL BELONGS IN CHURCH

Right now we have twinges of conscience and know that we can petition God for forgiveness of those sins; but what if we were constantly fearing that a voice from heaven would boom, "Busted!" or an angel would poke us with a sword every time we cussed when we stubbed a toe, every time we envied another person, every time we made up excuses for skipping work?

Only extreme masochists would enjoy that sort of world and God wouldn't enjoy **putting** us in that sort of world.

Accept it by faith that God is doing the best He can...**under the current circumstances**.

Someday when there is a new heaven and a new earth, when there are unbounded resources, when Christians have been purged of their old lusts, when the people who really, really don't want to live in the presence of God have been sent into outer darkness, **then** there will be a cessation of death, sorrow, and crying (Revelation 21:4 – my favorite verse in the Bible).

In the meantime, we have a responsibility for making the best of an imperfect world – helping the widows, the orphans, the handicapped, and others who are in need. Some of us are already doing an admirable job, but all of us could probably do at least a little more.

A committed Christian outlook is well-suited to these demands.

You can assert that the presence of evil and suffering in the world "proves" the nonexistence of God, but that assertion does not cure a single blind orphan.

You can say that God is an incompetent klutz because he doesn't retrofit the world to **your** liking, but that declaration does not dig a single well for thirsty villagers.

Yes, Your Butt STILL BELONGS IN CHURCH

You can scream that God is a heartless monster because he does not wipe away all tears **right now**, but that does not provide a single meal.

Yes, non-Christian or non-religious people can (and do) carry out impressive humanitarian projects.

But nothing – except willful pride and obstinance – prevents those humanitarian projects from being carried out **in conjunction with the Gospel message**.

Satan has already **caused** sin, death, and suffering in the world; don't let him use a slanted view of those conditions to trick you into giving up on a blissful eternity.

Excuse 5: "God took my momma"

Because of a misunderstanding about the nature of life and death, many people harbor a lifelong grudge against God.

Because God "took" one of their loved ones, they hate him until their dying day.

(Yes, this is a more personalized offshoot of the "sin and suffering" excuse. I decided to give it a chapter of its own.)

Agreed, the Bible tells of the earth swallowing up Israelites who defied God. It tells of God sparing Daniel from the lion's den.

Fervent prayers **can** encourage God to guide the hands of surgeons and extend the life of patients who had a 10 percent chance of survival.

But God usually takes a much more **passive** role in the affairs of men.

Images of the Grim Reaper in popular culture (and perhaps faint memories of the Fates in Norse mythology weaving – and cutting – the tapestry of our lives) have conditioned us to think that God micromanages our departure time.

There is no scriptural basis for this.

Yes, Your Butt STILL BELONGS IN CHURCH

Bill Cosby's Cliff Huxtable character endeared himself to millions by telling his smug son Theo, "I brought you into this world – and I can take you out of it." Even more so, God has the **right** to make such declarations; but I find nothing to indicate that he is so capricious or impulsive. Maybe I'm being heretical here, but I think mostly He lets things run their course.

On a day to day basis, people wind up in the cemetery because we all eventually wear out, because someone was texting while driving, because someone brought a lethal virus into an environment, because someone didn't watch their diet, etc.

And **if** God does choose to deliberately "take" someone, there is no scriptural basis for saying He was evil or unjustified in doing it. **Maliciousness** is solely in the eye of the beholder.

If your mother or your cousin or your old coach is in a right relationship with God when God (or natural causes or an accident or murder) "takes" them, they are only transitioning to an infinitely better place. And if they **aren't** in a right relationship with God, that's on **them**.

If your loved one was a decent, God-fearing person, do you think they would be **proud** of you for brooding, cursing God, and avoiding Christian companionship? What sort of **legacy** are you leaving if your bitterness influences your children, grandchildren, great-grandchildren…?

Remember the stereotypical scene from martial arts movies? An egotistical novice thinks he's going to be a superstar in hand-to-hand combat from the get-go, but the wise old sensei hands him his butt.

If the novice is the star of the movie (rather than a supporting character), he will **eventually** learn his lesson: being the slave of **emotions** (anger, pride, hatred, fear) will always leave you at a disadvantage with your

Yes, Your Butt STILL BELONGS IN CHURCH

opponent. When you calmly focus on the **goal**, then you can achieve incredible success.

People who rage against God have **two** enemies to take into consideration. First, they are their own worst enemy. Second, Satan is laughing himself silly as they move farther and farther from God's light.

You can stew in your bitterness. You can scapegoat God over an accident, a crime, or a poor lifestyle choice. But letting those raw emotions dominate your life will not help you to focus on the goal of reaching heaven.

I am sorry if the grief counseling you received was inadequate – or if you never sought any grief counseling to start with. It's worth trying and trying again to get in a right relationship with God (and to be a more pleasant person to be around on Earth).

Whether or not God chooses to tinker with the details of your life, He is still in charge. No matter what kind of tough guy you are, someday you will **answer** to Him.

If you have cut off your nose to spite your face, you may not **smell** the fire and brimstone, but you will certainly feel their effects.

Make the dear departed proud of you and stop blaming God.

Excuse 6:

"Church attendance is no guarantee of getting to heaven"

Not every wavering Christian, lapsed Christian, or never-Christian appreciates country music; but most of them would probably take solace in the romantic ballad *I Believe in You,* by the late Don Williams.

That's because one of the lines in the song is the populist sentiment "I don't believe that heaven waits for only those who congregate."

"He's right!" they'll chime in. "Not everyone who goes to church is going to heaven, and some people who aren't in church **will** make it to heaven."

Some parts of that declaration are definitely true and some are debatable, but how one **applies** those ideas is crucial.

For starters, agreed, it's painfully obvious that not every pew-occupier meets the high standards set by God.

Yes, Your Butt STILL BELONGS IN CHURCH

God commands us to worship **in spirit and in truth** (John 4:24). So, the people who engage in razzle-dazzle Christianity-on-steroids (but who openly flout certain requirements) are not going to make it into eternal rest.

As for the legalists who cross every "t" and dot every "I": if they have lost their enthusiasm for Christ and do not **love** their fellow man, **their** worship is in vain.

Let's look at four examples of **secular** issues that parallel the "not everyone who goes to church is going to heaven" argument.

Not everyone who gets vaccinated for flu escapes getting the flu. Some people who **skip** the vaccine still manage to make it through the winter without getting sick.

Not everyone who strives to do well in school gets a high-paying job. Some dropouts **do** get a high-paying job.

Sometimes someone will feed incorrect data into a GPS database. Since "even a blind hog finds an acorn every now and then," sometimes drivers stumble across their destination **without** the use of GPS or a paper map.

Not everyone who wears a seatbelt survives a car crash. Everyone has a "friend of a friend" anecdote about someone who survived a crash because they **weren't** strapped in.

But...science shows that vaccinations greatly increase your odds of **avoiding** or **moderating** an illness.

A high school diploma or college degree is not a **guarantee** of a lucrative job, but it certainly improves your odds and your **flexibility**. (Most of the dropouts who prosper do so because of an athletic skill or some narrowly focused blue-collar talent. If they become permanently disabled or automation makes their skills obsolete, they are stuck with few options.)

Yes, Your Butt STILL BELONGS IN CHURCH

By and large, utilizing GPS or a printed map will greatly increase your chance of getting to the right place in a timely fashion.

Anecdotes and rebellious streaks aside, statistics clearly show the value of "buckling up" before pulling onto the road.

Back to church attendance. No, getting your hand stamped at the door does not mean you are guaranteed entrance into heaven. But if your religion is scripturally sound and you look forward to associating with like-minded individuals, you greatly increase your chances of staying steadfast and being pleasing to the Almighty.

Let's turn to the issue of the fate of those outside the church.

You'll occasionally see a picture of a student who made it through 13 years of primary and secondary education without a single day of absence. But I don't know that there has ever been an adult who has never missed a day of church.

And I have found no scripture indicating that God will surprise you on Judgment Day with a gleeful shout of "Aha! My records indicate that you failed to stay for the entirety of evening worship on the third Sunday of July in 2009. Welcome to the lake of fire!"

God created the Human Condition, so God **understands** the Human Condition. He knows there will be times (one-off or prolonged) when it is impossible or unwise to gather with dozens, hundreds, or thousands of other worshippers in familiar, formal surroundings.

You may be hospitalized in a body cast or hooked up to a life-support system. You may have a seriously compromised immune system and avoid large gatherings -- or may have a contagious disease and wish to spare

Yes, Your Butt STILL BELONGS IN CHURCH

others. God understands that livestock can tear down fences on Sunday morning and endanger both motorists and the rancher's life savings.

Soldiers in foxholes may have to settle for the next time combat allows them to chat with the chaplain. An astronaut may have to worship on his own because he's thousands of miles above his home congregation. A missionary may spend weeks trekking to his remote destination, and even then will probably worship in a meager hut instead of the sort of church building we take for granted.

Stuff happens. God understands.

But the examples I've given do not excuse the other cases.

God's patience grows thin when week after week, month after month, year after year you avoid church because...you got out of the habit or you found something more entertaining or that old lady looked funny at you or...

Much of humanity's misery comes from the "It can't happen to me" conceit. People marry mates who are known cheaters, skip backing up their computer files, falsify their tax returns, and drink to excess because it's always someone **else** who gets cheated on, suffers a computer crash, gets audited, or develops cirrhosis of the liver.

Can you say, "in denial"? Such philosophies of life are presumptuous and foolhardy. And it's just as presumptuous and foolhardy to **assume** that you will be one of the lucky ones that God cuts extra slack.

Lax worshippers are emboldened by "What about...?" questions. You know, like "What about the heart-of-gold guy in a remote village of idol-worshipping cannibals, who knows something isn't right and is sincerely seeking the Truth -- but has never been reached by a missionary and thus has never seen a Bible or even heard the name of Jesus Christ?"

God is merciful. God is fair. While we continue trying to **minimize** the number of people worldwide who have never heard the Gospel preached, God has the authority to deal with this hypothetical villager as He sees fit. Trust Him.

But it takes a tremendous amount of gall to use this hard case as an excuse for those who willfully reject church attendance.

God judges us according to the resources and opportunities we possess. ("But he that knew not, and did commit things worthy of stripes, shall be beaten with few stripes. For unto whomsoever much is given, of him shall be much required: and to whom men have committed much, of him they will ask the more." – Luke 12:48)

Most of the people reading this book will have a church within a few miles of their home. They will have their own vehicle or someone willing to transport them to worship services. They will have spent a lifetime with inexpensive Bibles and study tools readily available.

So, it is a shameful dereliction of duty to hold up a remote villager as an excuse for not regularly worshipping in America or some other First World society.

If God chooses to make an exception for a sincere seeker of Truth (and there **are** sticklers who insist, "Sorry, remote villager, you absolutely **must** be saved in the name of Jesus"), that offers absolutely no excuse for someone who willfully neglects/avoids public worship.

Yes, Your Butt STILL BELONGS IN CHURCH

Excuse 7:
"Sunday is my one day a week to sleep in"

Although many would-be Christians treat "Sunday is my one day a week to sleep in" (delivered with a self-pitying grin) as a self-evident truth ("Duh!"), my exhaustive research finds no mandate for such a practice in our major religious, political, or scientific papers.

The guarantee of slumbering until brunch-time is found nowhere in the Bible (Old Testament or New). It's not in the Declaration of Independence, the United States Constitution, the Magna Carta, the Declaration of the Rights of Man, Einstein's Special Theory of Relativity, or any sort of definitive document I can track down.

Certainly, mothers, doctors, and teachers sing the praises of "getting enough sleep"; but it's pure wishful thinking to translate that as "catch up on sleep on the Lord's Day."

Allowances have to be made for insomnia or medical emergencies or pulling an "all-nighter"; but I think most reputable health experts recommend the ideal of getting sufficient sleep **each night** – not habitually skimping and then grabbing an extra four or five hours on Saturday night.

God programmed our circadian rhythms into us. It would be extremely short-sighted of Him to include a desperate need to get 40 winks on Sunday morning.

When I hear "Sunday is my one day a week to sleep in," my gut instinct is to issue some profane variation on "Boo hoo"; but I shall try to be more sympathetic and genteel.

My more constructive response is to opine that it sounds like a **time-management problem** to me.

Yes, there are people who must juggle a full-time job and four part-time jobs to make ends meet. (Sometimes this is just how the dice rolls, and sometimes it is the result of an accumulation of bad life choices.) Some people are run ragged seeing to the needs of neglected grandchildren and/or aging parents. There are people (especially in the sports and entertainment fields) who are routinely up way past midnight on weekends.

On the other hand, there are people who need to **de-clutter their lives** and decide the things that are truly important in life. Do you really have to attend every performance within a 250-mile radius by your favorite B-list band? Would the coach get laid off if you occasionally missed a game of your favorite team? Do you really have to enroll your children in every extracurricular activity imaginable? Are you really on an immutable, life-or-death deadline to binge-watch every episode of a hot new streaming series that someone at work mentioned?

I am reminded of a line by the character Phoebe Buffay in the TV series *Friends*. Someone needed a favor from Phoebe, but she replied, "Gee, I **wish** I could help you, but I don't **want** to." That's the attitude many of us have about Sunday worship. We wish we could get up early

Yes, Your Butt STILL BELONGS IN CHURCH

enough to shower, dress, and get to the house of worship — but we don't genuinely **want** to (or at least not enough to kick the habit of staying up too late on Saturday night).

Think about it. If people finally get all their children to move out or settle their parents' estate or land a job with a much shorter commute, how often is their **first impulse** "Yeehaw! Now we can spend more time on **church**!"?

People tend to shed **crocodile tears** about not making it to church. The people who regret not making it to Sunday morning services also turn down the chance to attend Sunday night services, Wednesday night services, home Bible studies, etc. The people who regret missing formal gatherings **might** be listening to inspirational audiobooks while commuting, but most likely they're listening to music, sports, or talk radio.

Many of the people who can't quite manage to wake up before noon on Sunday would leap at the chance to get up at the crack of dawn in order to grab the best fishing spot, beat traffic to the gun-and-knife expo, stand in line for concert tickets, or meet an old college friend for brunch. This shows their priorities.

Some people are so brash as to insist that they have "earned" their one day a week to sleep late. You can earn wages from your boss. You can behave in a manner that earns the respect of your neighbors. But the notion that God (who gave us our lives and all the wonders of nature and the blood of His only begotten Son) still **owes** us something is ludicrous. He is faithful to uphold His promises, but those promises derive from grace and love, not because God is **dependent** on us. No, we cannot "earn" the right to skip out on worshiping God.

The idea of one-day-a-week-to-sleep-in is part of the idiocy that drifts through the collective consciousness of mankind. You know, like "You can't get pregnant the first

Yes, Your Butt STILL BELONGS IN CHURCH

time," "You can't get pregnant standing up," "If you cross your fingers, it's not really a lie," "Finders keepers, losers weepers," and "If it doesn't touch the ground more than five seconds, you can still eat it."

You don't get to beg off by saying, "I guess I'm just not a morning person." The early Christians didn't take the easy way out by saying, "I guess I'm just not a getting-fed-to-the-lions person." Without the convenience of alarm clocks, blow dryers, SUVs, and a First Amendment guarantee of freedom of worship, they got up, groomed themselves, made it to an assembly place (a church building, a synagogue, the home of a member, the catacombs, wherever), and worshipped the Lord together, even in the face of persecution.

My son (the future engineer) grew up with a pipe dream of inventing a time machine. Too bad we don't have such a device. I could take a group of "one day to sleep in" folks back to the first century to share their sad story with the first Christian converts.

On second thought, it might not go over so well.

Excuse 8:

"The church is full of hypocrites"

Yes, this one is such a classic that it was hard not to start with it.

This excuse has been a handy fallback for way too long.

For one thing, it is a shameful example of **stereotyping**, just as much as saying "All blondes are ditzy" or "All Republicans are heartless" or "All African-Americans are lazy" or "All Mexicans are rapists."

Most people who employ this excuse haven't really done the heavy lifting of compiling an exhaustive list of hypocritical behavior. They pick one or two prominent Christians who haven't met their exacting standards and extrapolate to say that the virus has spread to everyone in the building.

Yes, there are two-faced people in church. There are people who are deceptive about little things, as well as people who harbor deep, dark secrets. Church camp counsellors sometimes molest campers. Deacons are sometimes spotted stumbling drunk on Saturday night. The person who gives you a hug may gossip about you all the way home.

Yes, Your Butt STILL BELONGS IN CHURCH

But it is a lie to say that church people have a **monopoly** or trademark on hypocrisy.

We are deluding ourselves when we insist that only "stuffed-shirt Bible thumpers" are capable of being hypocritical. We pretend that non-Christians are an open book. "They're keeping it real. What you see is what you get. They're not pretending to be anything they're not. They let you see them warts and all. They've dropped all pretense. Their motives are transparent."

Bunk.

The "real world" outside the church doors is rife with white lies, half-truths, exaggerations, repressed emotions, mixed motives, manipulations, bluffs, and self-serving scams.

Whether for selfish reasons or altruistic reasons, people **in general** aren't always what they seem.

You may know your poker buddy is a womanizer, but that doesn't mean you realize he is specifically trying to seduce **your** wife.

You may know that a friend drinks a lot, but that doesn't mean he isn't hiding a cirrhosis diagnosis from you. He may be the life of the party, but he may be lonely and depressed when you're not watching.

If you're 16 with an i.d. that says you were born 21 years ago, isn't that a part of pretending to be something you're not?

Sucking in your gut, wearing makeup, wearing contact lenses, dyeing your hair, undergoing hair-implant surgery, getting breast implants, getting Botox injections: these are all ways of fooling people about the hand Mother Nature (and bad habits) has dealt you.

Yes, Your Butt STILL BELONGS IN CHURCH

You may lie to your spouse or a friend about their physical appearance or a purchase they've made, just to keep from hurting their feelings.

Just to keep a paycheck, people will pretend to respect a boss they consider to be an idiot and a tyrant.

Just to keep peace in the extended family, you may act cordial around in-laws you absolutely loathe.

You don't have to be a churchgoer in order to let someone think your painstakingly selected wardrobe is something you just happened to throw on ("This old rag?"), or that your home is always that spotless.

Tough guys who were taught "Big boys don't cry" may be real softies at heart.

When someone tells you "I'm fine," that doesn't guarantee you can take their reassurances at face value; sometimes they just don't want to burden others with their emotional/marital/illness/financial problems.

Christmas letters are notorious for painting a far rosier picture than exists in reality. Those letters are not exclusively written by Christians.

I could go on and on, but I think you get the idea.

Hypocrisy is part of the human condition, not just the Christian condition.

Yes, Christians should be held to a higher standard, but not an **impossibly** high standard.

I wish someone could explain to me why Christians must be singled out as pariahs. It's supposedly excruciatingly painful to spend two hours occupying a pew with a fallible Christian — but we spend hours and hours with a co-worker who desperately fakes being competent, a neighbor who is pretends to be a big shot while struggling to avoid bankruptcy court, a chum who strings together bald-faced lies to meet women, etc.

I'm not the first person to point out the short-sightedness of using hypocrites as an excuse. If a Christian really is a hypocrite, he will have to answer to God for that. If he dies unrepentant, he will go to hell. And if you give up your spiritual moorings to avoid sitting with that Christian, whenever you die, you will most likely be condemned to hell.

And you will be spending **all eternity** with the very people you couldn't bear to be around for a few hours.

What sense does that make?

Excuse 9:
"Church people have let me down"

This excuse is a sort of continuation of the "hypocrites" gambit.

I'm not going to deny that sometimes Christians are self-absorbed and let opportunities slip through the cracks.

And we shouldn't. In Galatians 6:9, Paul stated, "And let us not be weary in well doing: for in due season we shall reap, if we faint not."

Furthermore, "Therefore to him that knoweth to do good, and doeth it not, to him it is sin." (James 4:17)

You really can't have too many sermons and Sunday school lessons about compassion, hospitality, humility, and self-sacrifice.

More often than I'd like to admit, I sum up my week by exclaiming something like, "Aaagggh! I clean forgot that funeral on Thursday! And I meant to buy some Girl Scout cookies from the Wilson girl on the back row. And we still haven't bought provisions to donate to the orphanage."

I always resolve to do a little better the next time, but life comes at you fast.

Yes, Your Butt STILL BELONGS IN CHURCH

If you're feeling neglected or marginalized by your brothers and sisters in Christ, please keep in mind that there's usually plenty of blame to spread around.

If you're getting more and more baffled during Bible class or during the sermon because you've never quite grasped certain terminology, **ask questions**.

If you try to slip into the auditorium and remain under the radar, you will probably **succeed** in staying under the radar. If you smile bravely and insist, "I'm doing fine," most people will take you at your word.

I know making assumptions can be dangerous ("When you assume, you make an ass out of 'u' and 'me'"), but it's **human nature** that folks – absent a cry for help – will assume that your needs are being met by your own grit, your family members, or social services (Meals on Wheels, the Welfare office, senior citizens bus, etc.)

Christians – especially working together as a team—can do many amazing things. But one feat they **can't** accomplish is **reading minds**.

If you're lonely, need a ride to a doctor's appointment, are feeling suicidal because you saw your ex with someone else, are no longer physically capable of mowing your own lawn, are struggling with your nicotine addiction, or can't quite come up with enough money for your utility bills, **say something**.

Be honest: when you've mingled at worship service, you've mostly thought things like, "I love that outfit! I wonder if I'd look good in something like that?" or "I hope he's not going to tell that same corny joke again" or "It sure is inspirational to see old lady Alexander here." You're probably **not** thinking, "I wonder if he's lonely, needs a ride to the doctor's appointment, feels suicidal because he saw his ex with someone else…"

Yes, Your Butt STILL BELONGS IN CHURCH

It may gall you to appear weak or needy, but it's better to speak up than to let secret resentments fester.

My mother, bless her heart, is one of those people who takes a **perverse pride** in being snubbed. Until the Covid-19 scare sidelined her (temporarily, I hope), she was always the first person in the church building on Sunday morning; but she has a propensity for **keeping score**. She rehashes who all didn't speak to her, forgot to bring some trinket they promised, didn't send a birthday card, etc. I am told that she'll never change, but it remains toxic behavior, nonetheless. She has a lack of empathy for the fact that other people all have their own life stories.

It's best to keep **reasonable expectations** of what fellow Christians will do for you. I'm sure that a handful of Christians **do** live "six-page Christmas letter" lives. They're independently wealthy or have highly flexible high-six-figure jobs. They have bottomless leisure time for yachting and tennis playing. Their jet-setting parents are still doing high-impact aerobics and parasailing in their nineties. The kids never need braces or eyeglasses and never get sick. Their servants fetch them mint juleps, transport the children to extracurricular activities, and arrange for the purchase of a new sports car when the ashtray gets full.

Most Christians – regardless of age, race, or social status – live **messier** lives than that. They have special needs children and/or aging parents who tend to break hips and catch pneumonia. They have long commutes and grueling jobs that leave them collapsing into a recliner at the end of the day. They have commitments to worthy causes such as the Lions Club, the Rotary Club, the Kiwanis Club, the PTO, or the Neighborhood Watch. They are still paying student loans and mortgages. They have pets to bury and trash to recycle and shingles to replace.

Yes, Your Butt STILL BELONGS IN CHURCH

Some Christians have more spare time than others. Some Christians have more talents or connections than others. But I think usually true Christians – if made aware of a need – will be only too glad to mow lawns, nail down loose boards, help you fill out a résumé, etc.

If you can set aside your wounded pride and assess your situation clearly, maybe you'll **still** conclude, "I was right— I **have** been surrounding myself with self-centered 'Christians' who don't care anything about me."

If that case, maybe it's best you move on and find a congregation that better appreciates you and better meets your unique needs.

But don't hold your negative experiences against all of Christianity.

Getting miffed about not having your physical/emotional needs met does not change your **spiritual** needs.

Yes, it's inexcusable that you have to sit for two hours in the doctor's waiting room – but even if you stomp away, that does not change the fact that you need your illness diagnosed and a prescription written. You may throw a tantrum because the grocery store is out of your favorite brand of salsa, but if you swear off grocery stores completely, you'll get hungry very quickly. Yes, that mechanic was rude to you; but if you burn rubber getting out of the garage without your vehicle being serviced, those faulty brakes could still cause a fatal accident.

To rehash the point from the previous chapter: Cut yourself off from Christian nourishment and you will eventually wind up spending **eternity** with cold-hearted "Christians" for whom you have lost all respect.

Yes, Your Butt STILL BELONGS IN CHURCH

Excuse 10:
"I don't want people knowing my business"

"I don't want people knowing my business."

That's one of the reasons someone dear to me has given for not darkening the doors of a church he left more than 30 years ago. (The doors of that church or any church building, for that matter.)

Put aside the fact that most of the individuals who might have been "watching" him or "judging" him probably died 10 or 20 years ago.

The whole idea of maintaining absolute privacy is a vain attempt to put the genie back in the bottle. In the Information Age, privacy is a ship that sailed long ago.

Sure, people may take a stab at privacy with gated communities, unlisted phone numbers, and tinted vehicle windows; but there's still a lot of information out there.

Many small-town newspapers regularly publish accounts of land transfers, divorces, and business incorporations. This

Yes, Your Butt STILL BELONGS IN CHURCH

is in addition to news items about domestic disputes, public drunkenness, and codes violations.

Websites such as "Find-A-Grave" let friends/acquaintances/strangers dig up all sorts of information about your ancestors.

Google Earth lets people on the other side of the world know almost as much about your surroundings as your next-door neighbor does.

Without your permission, former classmates you barely remember can post a photo of "Mrs. McGillicuddy's Sixth Grade Class" and let everyone see just how dorky you looked way back when.

Unless you're conscientious about scrubbing your internet presence clean, "cookies" will let companies know everything you've purchased and every topic you've researched.

So, considering the lack of privacy in general, I'm not sure why people feel compelled to harp on church members "knowing my business."

To make things even more exasperating, many of the folks who are worried about people knowing their business don't have anything particularly scandalous in their lives. They just start out with a combative, chip-on-the-shoulder attitude.

I am not going to lie to you. Busybodies, gossips, and well-meaning meddlers do exist within the church.

But avoiding church altogether because of them will do nothing to improve their perception of you. Hiding will only "prove" that they were right to be suspicious of you. It's better to "kill" them with kindness.

And please be open to the notion that maybe the vast majority of Christians **don't** keep a dossier on you.

Yes, Your Butt STILL BELONGS IN CHURCH

Growing up in the rural South, I've grown quite accustomed to people (both inside and outside the church) asking things such as "How are you doing?," "What have you been up to this week?," and "Did y'all ever find a renter for your momma's house?"

Some of the queries are heart-felt and some are undoubtedly perfunctory chitchat ("Must make sure I speak to everyone, even those I don't know very well"), but I try to give people the benefit of the doubt.

If you bristle at every question...if you try to twist every good-will gesture into a backhanded compliment...if you are constantly reading between the lines in search of subtext and ulterior motives...**sounds like a personal problem to me!**

I thought we had all agreed that slavery is bad. Stop being a slave to paranoia!

Yes, Your Butt STILL BELONGS IN CHURCH

Excuse 11:

"I can read the Bible at home"

Although some workplaces have gotten nervous about "open carry" of religious books and symbols, for the most part, it's **undeniably true** that you can read the Bible in places other than a church building.

I'll refrain from sliding into Dr. Seuss-like rhyming, but you can flip open the Good Book almost anywhere: in your den, in your bedroom, in your backyard, in your car, in the park...

My contention is that such reading should be a **supplement** to public worship, not a **replacement** for it.

(Please note that I am not addressing people who are confined to a hospital bed or dealing with a severely compromised immune system. Nor am I talking about people who live in the middle of nowhere, with no church available except a cult that's waiting for the lizard people to return from Alpha Centauri. I'm talking about able-bodied people who have viable options available to them but simply **choose** not to engage in public worship.)

Yes, Your Butt STILL BELONGS IN CHURCH

Obviously, you're not getting enough out of your solitary Bible study if it doesn't **inspire** you to associate with other Bible readers.

Unless you're **extremely** introverted, germophobic, or misanthropic, human beings **enjoy** group experiences for things that are truly important to them.

Depending on their individual interests and hobbies, people normally **enjoy** hosting the Wednesday afternoon book club, admiring the vintage automobiles of other car collectors at the local Sonic drive-in, attending VFW meetings, bringing a potluck dish to the monthly Retired Teachers Association get-together, dressing up for a comic book convention, etc. Not everyone will be the proverbial "first to arrive and the last to leave," but people generally like spending at least a little time with like-minded individuals.

Contrary to popular belief, not even homeschoolers live in a bubble. They often pool their resources for intermural sports events or joint field trips.

I've lost count of how many times our minister has opened a lesson by quoting King David from Psalm 122: "I was glad when they said unto me, Let us go into the house of the LORD." If gladness is **not** one of the emotions that comes to mind when you think about a centralized place of worship, you need to ask yourself **why**.

So, if you're **not** itching to get with other Bible readers, could it be that Bible reading isn't truly **important** to you?

Or is there some other psychological factor standing in your way? Perhaps an **inferiority complex** makes you loathe to go around people who will have fancier clothing and automobiles. In that case, you should either give those people a **chance** to treat you as an equal or try attending a more down-to-earth, laid-back congregation. Or perhaps

Yes, Your Butt STILL BELONGS IN CHURCH

it's plain old **pride** that makes you think you couldn't possibly learn anything from those hicks who show up every Sunday. Church is a good place to learn humility. I'm just saying.

Maybe you're just addicted to your **comfort zone**. When I was a little kid in church, we belted out the song "I've got the love of Jesus, love of Jesus, love of Jesus down in my heart." Such a sentiment pays better long-term dividends than "I've got the love of Haagen-Dazs and bunny slippers down in my heart."

If your solitary Bible study brings you brilliant insights about God, it's **selfish** of you not to share those insights with other Christians. If your solitary Bible study **doesn't** bring you brilliant insights, maybe that's a sign it's **not working**.

Bible study is challenging, but it is a **different type** of challenge depending on whether you're studying alone or studying in a group. When you're reclining in your easy chair, it can be challenging to interpret Old Testament metaphors, slog through tedious details of ceremonial law, or grasp Paul's deeper theological contentions. (Not to mention challenging to resist the siren call of distractions such as Amazon shopping, channel surfing, and your ball-chasing terrier.) When you're in a group that condenses and clarifies and raises relatable contemporary applications of 2,000-year-old principles, you can find your **preconceived notions** challenged.

"Practice makes perfect," goes the maxim. It should be "**Perfect** practice makes perfect." If you practice something wrong ("The normal human body temperature is 96-point-8"), you will **learn** it wrong. Studying on your own, you may totally misunderstand an archaic key word in a passage every time you read it, or drum into your consciousness that a particular passage is literal instead of symbolic.

Yes, Your Butt STILL BELONGS IN CHURCH

Surely, I am not the only worshipper who has heard someone say, "I've read that verse a hundred times over the years, and I've never really thought about it that way until **now**."

I'll give you the benefit of the doubt. Maybe you **can** miraculously glean everything you need from studying the Bible all by your lonesome. But you owe it to **weaker brethren** to take **their** welfare into consideration. You should inspire them to be **better** people, not more complacent people.

Yes, you run the risk of being an obstacle and an enabler for those who are less able to understand and implement Bible teachings. ("If Matilda can stay at home on Sundays and be a good Christian, so can I. It'll give me more time to get over my hangover, too.")

Communal study is mutually rewarding. Daily Bible study should be the **icing on the cake**, not the totality of your diet.

Excuse 12:

"Communing with nature does me just as much good as church"

Many people will tell you that they get their Recommended Daily Requirement of worship while doing activities in the Great Outdoors – golfing, jogging, hiking a mountain trail, birdwatching, enjoying a beautiful sunset, etc.

Perhaps I am being impertinent, but I am compelled to wonder which came first: the desire to serve God or the desire to do outdoors-y things.

Nearly 20 years ago I saw a "News of the Weird"-type news item about Christian nudists and satirized the idea in one of my newspaper columns. Christian nudists unleashed their wrath.

My most charitable interpretation of the hate mail was **not** that these Christians had a sudden epiphany and realized that wearing clothes to church was **wrong** and that God would be much more pleased if they got "nekkid." No, it seems either they were nudists to start with or they were

Yes, Your Butt STILL BELONGS IN CHURCH

Christians whose curiosity was piqued by nudity and who went about **defensively retrofitting** their lifestyle into God's plan.

Similarly, I wonder how many of the Great Outdoors worshippers have truly discovered that golfing, jogging, hiking, birdwatching, and enjoying sunsets are the absolute best way to please God and secure their eternal salvation.

Is it possible that these people just like golfing, jogging, hiking, birdwatching, and enjoying sunsets and are trying to shoehorn their spirituality into it? ("Oh, yeah, and I feel closer to God and His Son What's-His-Name every time I stick a worm on a hook. Yeah – that's the ticket.")

God created nature: the hills, mountains, rivers, lakes, stars, moons, etc. He declared his creation to be "good." He intends for the wonders of nature to be one of the evidences for His existence.

But such things are not meant to be idols or the **focus** of our worship. In chapter 1 of Romans, Saint Paul condemned those who "changed the truth of God into a lie, and worshipped and served the creature more than the Creator."

The instructions supplied by nature are terribly imprecise, compared to what you can get by reading and discussing the Bible. Precision can be crucial.

Imagine you're on your first day of work at a new job. Instead of listening to the instructions from the supervisor who is teaching you the ropes, you meander around all slack-jawed, marveling at the awesomeness of the merchandise, equipment, or software.

Depending on the job, you may wind up violating the dress code, flagrantly breaking sexual harassment rules, deleting irreplaceable files before backing them up, leaving your biggest client fuming while you finish telling a co-worker a

Yes, Your Butt STILL BELONGS IN CHURCH

long-winded anecdote, not knowing which doors you're responsible for locking, extending credit to a would-be customer everyone else knows is a bad risk, flipping a front-end loader, losing a few fingers, or at best remaining blissfully ignorant of your benefits package.

Mere awe and adoration get you only so far in personal relationships as well. Your spouse probably appreciates your gazing at them lovingly, commenting on their beautiful voice, or giving them a playful slap on the buttocks. But…

But if you're too busy being googly-eyed and "in love with being in love," you're probably failing to process and remember the actual words they speak to you.

So there's probably a big fight brewing when you forget to pick up milk on the way home, disregard explicit instructions not to track mud into the house, fail to pass along news that your spouse's doctor appointment has been rescheduled, etc.

If your absent-mindedness is a **habitual** behavior, no amount of flirting is going to patch up your marriage.

If you go to the automotive dealership to purchase a new sports car and spend all your time drooling over the vehicle and listening to Steppenwolf's *Born To Be Wild* in your mind, while ignoring everything the salesman says (about the formulation of oil to use, the required maintenance schedule, the recall notice on the airbags, and the interest on overdue payments), you may be in for a rude awakening.

The devil is in the details – and the devil is anxious for you to **overlook** the details.

My reading of the Bible (Genesis through Revelation) reveals a God who delivers specific instructions with specific consequences. Awe of nature is extra.

Yes, Your Butt STILL BELONGS IN CHURCH

Religious bodies have enough disagreements over issues such as abortion and capital punishment even when they have the written scriptures. How are we supposed to get any practical advice from admiring nature? One person might see the "purple mountain majesties" and think "Wow! And heaven will be even better than this!" while another sees the mountains and sings, "Sha la la la la live for today!" Both cannot be right.

And if you spend all your time watching female praying mantises bite the heads off of their mates, how exactly does that translate into moral/ethical standards for relating to your Significant Other and your business associates????

I have no objection to a Sunday school class moving outdoors on a nice summer day. Before my congregation built a structure more than a hundred years ago, outdoor "brush arbor meetings" were held on the site. But they were **actual worship services** using hymns and sermons – not free-form wandering about, hoping to obtain Christianity by osmosis.

Even if you are the **one-in-a-billion** person who can **somehow** absorb everything he needs to know about God by tiptoeing through the tulips, you still carry the burden of **setting a good example** for the weaker brethren. The people who love and respect you may think they are as attuned to God as you are and go through the motions of copying your outdoor activities, but fall hideously short of attaining the same enlightenment.

Why do people let down their defenses around issues of alternative spirituality? Normally, we raise a skeptical eyebrow around things that seem too good to be true. ("Okay, what's the catch?") But let someone offer religion with no rules, regulations, or expectations (except "Bring sunscreen and mosquito spray") and suddenly it's "Where do I sign up???"

Yes, Your Butt STILL BELONGS IN CHURCH

Do not let Satan turn this into an **either/or** situation. Attending a formal worship service does not preclude you from additionally frolicking in the streams and meadows. But **settling** for the frolicking **can** preclude you from going to heaven.

Excuse 13:
"Meditation meets my spiritual needs"

Don't expect me to come down hard on meditation **per se**.

Although I enjoy being around fellow Christians at church, catching up on the watercooler talk at work, or spending five minutes chatting with old acquaintances at Walmart, I do "love me some solitude."

Some people can't be happy unless they're on a crowded dance floor, huddling in the bleachers with 50,000 other fans, or "hoisting a few" with other patrons of a watering hole; but I find my "alone time" priceless.

I hate not being able to hear myself think. I'm not alone. Among the things singer Mary Chapin Carpenter thinks she deserves in the country song *Passionate Kisses* are "Pens that won't run out of ink/And cool quiet and time to think."

Getting out from under the microscope and spending time with my thoughts can provide both relaxation and inspiration. I find clarity and bursts of creativity.

Yes, Your Butt STILL BELONGS IN CHURCH

Medical science shows that meditation can lower blood pressure and cause observable changes in brain waves.

Paul recommended meditation and deep thought in Philippians 4:8 ("Finally, brethren, whatever things are true, whatever things are noble, whatever things are just, whatever things are pure, whatever things are lovely, whatever things are of good report, if there is any virtue and if there is anything praiseworthy – meditate on these things.")

But there is only so much we can accomplish with meditation if the Bible is **not** part of the equation.

It's like the data processing philosophy of GIGO ("Garbage in, garbage out"). If all you're doing in your quiet moments is endlessly recirculating your own lusts ("Wow! I hope that waitress is wearing the tight blouse the next time I go to eat!"), shortsighted advice from your friends ("If I was you, I'd tell that tyrant of a boss to kiss my rear end!"), or snippets of songs and movie dialogue, meditation is no more a genuine substitute for public worship than digging up ginseng is.

And it's not just freeform meditating that is troublesome.

If you're taking **instruction** from some goofball who works as a self-styled **meditation guru** (between gigs as an Uber driver and operating a Pooper Scooper behind the dogs he walks), you should be asking yourself why **his** instruction is any more valid than the Bible's. Why are **his** credentials any better than those of the apostles who were martyred for the cause of Christ? ("Um, he's **cool** – and exotic!")

Is it **really** a good idea to tell people, "The answer is within yourself"? **Sociopaths** and **psychopaths** have answers within themselves, but they are not necessarily good answers. We need some standard of conduct **outside** ourselves.

I'll admit it: like the trust-building couples exercise of falling backward and letting your partner catch you, it **does** take a lot of faith for our finite brains to accept that there is a God who transcends space and time and has our best interests at heart; but it makes a heck of a lot **more sense** than the alternatives.

If you're supposed to relax, open your mind, and "become one with the universe," how exactly is "the universe" supposed to understand you and the human condition?

We focus on the sacrifice Jesus made during the crucifixion, but there was so much more to His earthly existence. Jesus was conceived and born. He doubtless grew up experiencing sibling rivalry, bullies, calloused hands, stubbed toes, hunger, thirst, disappointments, betrayals, the deaths of friends and loved ones (we know that Jesus's cousin John the Baptist was beheaded during Jesus's ministry), and abstaining from pleasures that were not part of His mission. Jesus knew what it was like to be human.

Jesus was no stranger to our infirmities. He can empathize with us. He knows none of us can live a flawless life, but He has proven that it is **more doable than we let on**.

And He has proven that it is possible to overcome death.

Now, how exactly does "the universe" understand what it's like to be human? What can we learn about morality and purpose from the asteroids, meteors, comets, moons, gas giants, etc.? Should we really settle for "What would the Crab Nebula do?" instead of "What would Jesus do?"

Even if you concede that there is some amorphous **sentience** to the material universe (and this falls into the "timey-wimey stuff" handy-dandy cop-out used for plot

Yes, Your Butt STILL BELONGS IN CHURCH

devices by the *Doctor Who* TV series), if this sentience demands something **less** or **different** than the demands in God's written word, how safe should you feel about tapping into that power?

Yes, you can light some incense candles, close your eyes, touch thumb to fingertip, and recite "Ommmm...."; but what assurance do you have that some constructive, worthwhile, **God-approved** information will be seeping into your skull?

How do you know it's not your inner longings, your guru's manipulations, or the direct power of Satan that is putting ideas into your head?

Is this not just man's willfulness, stubborn pride, and fruitless quest for the novel in action?

Most of us understand that being acceptable to God involves study, sacrifice, and obeying the rules. If one can just **passively** receive everything he needs for completeness, that sounds too good to be true – and we all know how such things usually turn out.

If there's **really** some sort of data transference going on with non-Christian meditation, let's look at it from a geopolitical standpoint: if the United States completely opened its borders, yes, there would be a lot of genuine refugees and good, hard-working people who would immigrate to our country. There would also be a large percentage of drug dealers, gang members, human traffickers, thieves, and permanently unemployed public wards.

And if you avoid the Bible and church and make your only contact with spirituality some ritualistic acceptance of whatever is poured into your head – no matter how many "levels" you obtain or new friends you make, your first face-to-face meeting with God will not be a pleasant one.

Yes, Your Butt STILL BELONGS IN CHURCH

Excuse 14:
"What I'm doing now is resonating with me just fine"

Resonate (verb): to resound; to produce a positive feeling, emotional response, or opinion.

"Resonate" is a word that gets tossed around casually nowadays.

When a speaker delivers an empty-calorie speech with a lot of carefully chosen buzzwords, audience members might respond, "That really resonates with me! He's speaking Truth to Power!"

When someone scrutinizes an atrocious, indecipherable piece of abstract art in a gallery and is fearful of admitting he doesn't "get" it, he's liable to gush, "That really resonates with me! It speaks to my soul!"

And many people use "resonate" to describe their appreciation for whatever they're using as a substitute for traditional religion.

Don't get me wrong. A place of worship **should** make you feel good. Using the "reasonable person" standard applied to many of our laws, a reasonable person should **not** have to feel threatened, unwelcome, or morally torn about being in a place of worship.

On the other hand, a "warm, fuzzy feeling" **by itself** is not a guarantee that one's choices (either secular or spiritual) are correct.

As Proverbs 14:12 explains, "There is a way which seemeth right unto a man, but the end thereof are the way of death."

Civilization prospers and advances when most of the people have a well-honed **conscience** and sense of community. It **falls apart** when most people have an attitude of "If it feels good, do it."

I am not here to dismiss the reality of hunches, notions, intuition, lucky guesses, premonitions, and gut instincts. I would just like to suggest that they be used **judiciously**.

Yes, some people have a phenomenal talent for picking winning stocks or bluffing at poker. But only a few people are so gifted; that's why their accomplishments are newsworthy or notable in the first place. And sometimes they humiliate themselves or lose a ton of money when they **guess wrong**.

Nowhere does God recommend that we worship Him or handle day-to-day situations purely on **emotion** and tingly sensations. In John 4:24, Jesus taught, "God is a Spirit: and they that worship him must worship Him in spirit and in truth." It's okay to be excited about a day trip with friends, but it's advisable to have a roadmap and a (moral) compass; declaring "That just **feels** like due north" is a recipe for disaster.

Mankind seems to possess a near-universal longing to return to childhood – before death, taxes, layoffs, bill collectors, and such things became **your** responsibility. Many people report the happiest times of their life as

Yes, Your Butt STILL BELONGS IN CHURCH

having been when they were sleeping in the back seat of the car while their parents drove them home at night.

Of course, these people should appreciate the fact that they are still **alive** and able to relate those warm childhood memories. Parents are not infallible or magically shielded; sometimes sleeping children die when an 18-wheeler jackknifes or a deer runs into a lane of traffic.

Similarly, we should not blithely entrust the **entirety** of our spiritual welfare to any single preacher, motivational speaker, self-help book, cute chick in the next cubicle, or internet mantra. We have a responsibility for evaluating the message and separating the wheat from the chaff.

There's nothing inherently wrong with seeking out surrogate parents (business mentors, kindly neighbors in a strange new town, co-workers who show us around); but we have to be grown-up enough to realize that we don't have the luxury of returning to the "back-seat cocoon." Sometimes people exploit us. Sometimes people mean well but get us into a trap of the blind leading the blind.

Proceed with caution when you encounter something and react with, "I can't put it into words, but it just feels good, it just feels right." Try a little **harder** to verbalize it. **Why** does it feel right? Because it corresponds to what God has listed as righteous behavior? Because it's the path of least resistance? Because it's something sparkly and new? Because all the trendsetters are doing it?

The answer to these questions matters. A lot.

"Buyer's remorse" works quite differently in earthly matters and spiritual matters. If you look at your new linoleum under a different light and decide you hate it, you can replace it, use a lot of throw rugs, or learn to live with it. If your child's "perfect" baby name gets him made fun of at school, you can switch to his middle name, use initials,

Yes, Your Butt STILL BELONGS IN CHURCH

or help him learn self-defense. If you discover that you and your Significant Other **aren't** really soulmates, you can put up with lowered expectations or part and learn to love again.

None of these are pleasant situations, but at least **life goes on**.

On the other hand, once you are facing **eternity**, you **can't** undo all the rash decisions that "seemed like a good idea at the time."

If you have been so prideful and arrogant that you insist on getting comfy-cozy with your "play it by ear" lifestyle, you will have an **infinite** amount of time to feel remorse for your irreversible snap judgments.

Excuse 15:

"I mean it: I'm happy with my alternatives"

This rationalization is closely connected to the last few excuses, but I'm exercising my prerogative to give it a little breathing space in a chapter of its own.

Nowadays, if anyone actually bothers to inquire about your religion at all, they probably wouldn't blink an eye if you confessed that you navigate the vagaries of life via astrology, palm reading, crystal ball gazing, seances, incense, earth goddesses, or some other mix-and-match conglomeration of guides – either as a supplement to traditional Christianity or as a **total replacement**.

In an increasingly secular world, you'll probably get a response of "Whatever floats your boat" or "Good for you!" It's sad that there aren't more people with the knowledge and courage to tell you that you're skating on thin ice.

As I remarked in an earlier chapter, if you have invested years of earnest study to become a dyed-in-the-wool devotee of any of these disciplines, I am not here to Change Your Life.

Yes, Your Butt STILL BELONGS IN CHURCH

But if you, or a loved one, or the next stranger you have a chance to influence are **dabbling** in such things and **depending** on such things, I feel obliged to share my thoughts on the matter.

Even if these beliefs provide a certain amount of comfort or motivation, they do not consider the Big Picture or offer a long-term answer to your problems.

Let me admit right up front that I have a healthy interest in the **paranormal**, dating even before 1971 when Granny Tyree died and I inherited her paperback copy of Frank Edwards' *Stranger Than Science*.

I have experienced enough, heard enough, and read enough to know that there are weird, unexplained things going on in the world – things that don't quite mesh either with known scientific laws **or** straitlaced religion.

Back in his bachelor days, my father avoided a head-on collision on a blind curve because he saw a vision that made him swerve to the right.

In her younger days, my mother went on a long road trip with her mother, her oldest brother, and his wife. My aunt had a premonition that they needed to pull off the road for a few minutes. When they proceeded, they came upon the aftermath of a wreck that they would have been right in the middle of.

Until his dying day, my mother's great-uncle told of an apparition he and his brother encountered in a field as youngsters.

My wife tells of spooky things that became almost the norm at her grandfather's ancestral home.

Both my father and my mother's aforementioned brother were able to "witch" water with a divining rod.

Yes, Your Butt STILL BELONGS IN CHURCH

When I was in elementary school, I was plagued by terrible warts on both hands. My father agreed to take me to a local man who allegedly possessed the mysterious power to cure such maladies. I woke up on the day we were scheduled to go visit him and all the warts had already completely vanished!

For two decades, my wife and I have achieved allergy relief through treatments based on Chinese acupuncture and the manipulation of the life force ("chi").

Government experiments indicate that some subjects can perform "remote viewing": seeing and hearing things in a closed room at a distance.

Research projects give credence to the concept of a "sixth sense" that gives you the "willies" when someone is looking at you behind your back.

If even a tiny fraction of the reports of Unidentified Flying Objects, reincarnation-implying incidents, and out-of-body experiences are true...

As the *X-Files* ads promised, "The truth is out there." I'm just not sure that the average person has the capacity to **glean and process** enough truth from today's trendy indulgences to withstand all of life's challenges. Honestly, a dalliance with alternative spirituality will probably give you **just enough knowledge to be dangerous**.

No alternative practice or combination of practices (offering a blood sacrifice under a full moon, paying a medium to put you into contact with your long-dead grandfather, sniffing exotic aromas, shuffling a deck of tarot cards, etc.) really prepares you to understand why the world exists, why you exist, what constitutes good and evil, and how to find peace and comfort in the afterlife.

Christianity is judged by unfair double standards. Its opponents pounce upon and magnify every instance of an

Yes, Your Butt STILL BELONGS IN CHURCH

avaricious preacher, a philandering deacon, or a member who blindly follows them. But when it comes to alternative spirituality, heaven forbid that anyone suggest there are charlatans, mental cases, overactive imaginations, wishful thinking, and followers who get in over their head.

Christianity's foes dispute even the most precise fulfilled prophecies, but get all excited over a vague horoscope that sort of kind of describes their day, or a sports team's winning streak that coincides perfectly with how long they've been wearing their sweaty team jersey without washing it.

Christianity's foes scoff at Christian concepts such as the Trinity, no matter how many times a believer explains them; but they go into "surfer dude" mode when some guru spouts some self-contradictory psychobabble. ("Dude, that is so **deep**!") Go read *The Emperor's New Clothes* if you want to learn more about such fawning.

In a later chapter, I will deal with nominal, immature Christians who are ill-prepared to defend their beliefs. For right now, we'll focus on the alternative spirituality people adherents.

Let's be blunt: some followers of alternative spirituality are downright goofy. Watch TV reality shows long enough, and you'll see what I mean. Bless their hearts, those people are adept at learning a Malaysian dance routine or rappelling down cliffs; but they show themselves to be mental lightweights when babbling about their "spirit animal," their "muse," or whatever superstition prods them to choose or not choose the number 13 during a contest.

Many forays into the occult are downright Satanic. Others may be benign ways to **waste time**. Even in a best-case scenario, none of them come close to building a firm foundation for being pleasing to God. If they happen to reveal a few kernels of good advice (even a blind hog finds an acorn every now and then), they are still merely shadows, echoes, and fragments of God's plan.

Even if there is a certain amount of truth attached to extrasensory perception, "urban legend" creatures, "talking to your inner child," "becoming one with the universe," or greeting "little green men," that does not mean traditional Christianity is outdated.

Lots of things **exist**. Archie comic books, old telephone directories, and mattress warning labels all **exist**; but that doesn't mean they provide all the ingredients for a successful lifestyle and philosophy.

Human beings are imbued with a deep-seated need for continuity, logic, and overarching themes. We are not designed for living lives of quiet desperation, playing hopscotch as we jump from "this hunch" to "that fortune cookie" to "a realistic dream I had last night" to "that sudden flareup of intuition" to...

Spirituality without Christianity is like trying to perform surgery with one hand tied behind your back.

Why, oh why, do people who are finicky about their mustard or their French film directors willingly accept inferior substitutes when it comes to spiritual matters?

Why – in a world with the song *Ain't Nothing Like the Real Thing, Baby* – do we gravitate away from the tried-and-true and toward something exotic?

Admit it: people suffer from a combination of ignorance, stubborn pride, and a never-ending quest for "doing cool stuff."

In Ecclesiastes 12:13, Solomon wrote, "Let us hear the conclusion of the whole matter: Fear God, and keep His commandments: for this is the whole duty of man."

Yes, Your Butt STILL BELONGS IN CHURCH

The whole duty of man. Yes, regardless of whether you're a new convert or a nonagenarian who was baptized as a teen, fearing/respecting God and keeping his commandments is a **full-time job.**

It really doesn't leave time for your other fears, anxieties, and worries.

There's no **time** for wondering, "Am I missing out on the latest self-help trend from the Hollywood glitterati?"

There's no **time** for wondering, "Am I infertile because I haven't found the right incantation yet?"

There's no **time** for worrying that your talismans aren't doing enough to stick it to the patriarchy.

There's no **time** for fretting that UPS may damage your latest batch of magic crystals.

The *Cliff's Notes* series has been a lifesaver for many a procrastinating high school English student, but a reader never quite gets the full impact of the original book, and many teachers have learned to ask questions that circumvent the themes discussed in Cliff's Notes.

Vitamin and mineral supplements are helpful for many people, but they can never fully make up for not getting a balanced diet containing fresh fruits and vegetables.

Would you hire an electrician who showed up for only every third class at trade school? Would you prepare for a high stakes spelling bee by studying only every other page of the dictionary? Would you commit to a date if your screen was fluttering and you could make out only one or two words of the other person's profile?

People who embrace alternative spirituality are falling for the same lie Satan used on Eve in the Garden of Eden. He told her that eating the forbidden fruit would make her as wise as God. Now he tells you that embracing an alternative spirituality will make you "smarter than those dumb ol' Christians."

Don't fall for it. He bedazzles you with the "Kellogg's Variety Pack," but he's luring you to an eternity of monotonous torment.

Yes, Your Butt STILL BELONGS IN CHURCH

Excuse 16:

"But I know what I'm doing"

When I was four years old, the formerly down-to-earth *Dick Tracy* comic strip swerved into a science fiction phase.

Industrialist Diet Smith developed the magnetism-powered "space coupe" and discovered Moon People with antennae, living in Moon Valley. Dick Tracy and the other cops ditched their patrol cars for magnetic air cars that resembled flying garbage cans.

These flying garbage cans gave me a bright idea. I would benevolently send my younger brother on a tour of the solar system. I even had a (not to scale) map of the planets drawn up. I found a glass jug of gasoline in the shed, and I just needed to figure out a way to attach it to the garbage can!

Of course, I was woefully ignorant of the volatility of gasoline, escape velocity, the airlessness of space, navigation concerns, reentry, and all that folderol; but it sure seemed like a good idea at the time.

My accident-waiting-to-happen was foiled when I strolled into the house and asked my father where we kept the

Yes, Your Butt STILL BELONGS IN CHURCH

matches. He looked up from his reading long enough to direct me to the correct drawer. Then he did a double-take. ("Matches? What does he need with **matches**???")

I know, I know. My wide-eyed misconceptions were understandable for a four-year-old boy. Since then I've graduated from public school (learning that Tom and Jerry cartoons do not constitute a physics curriculum), passed my driving test, earned a bachelor's degree, held down a couple of long-term jobs, voted, paid taxes, gotten married, and raised a precocious son of my own.

Still… youth is not the only reason for making bad decisions. Even now I could underestimate an opponent's ability to arm-wrestle. I could be talked into making a stupid purchase. I could be guilted into accepting a committee assignment that is way out of my league. I could guess wrong by half a million dollars concerning how much money I would need for a comfortable retirement.

I'm not perfect and I will always have things to learn, but after 45 years as a Christian, after decades of study – I feel reasonably secure in what Christianity offers.

On the other hand, if I went from zero to 60 and instantly found the same degree of comfort in a brand of spirituality espoused by a B-list actor in a late-night infomercial, I would be a darned fool.

I'm sorry but placing your reliance on occult mumbo jumbo is about as reasonable as my insisting, "Well, Dick Tracy went into outer space in the funny papers!"

Be honest with yourself. If you can truly say, "100% of the bright ideas I've dreamed up over the years have panned out," go ahead and **enjoy** your Ouija board, your daily horoscope, your rabbit's foot.

If you can't quite make that claim, come back to the solid rock that is the Gospel.

Yes, Your Butt STILL BELONGS IN CHURCH

Stop playing with matches.

Excuse 17:

"I'm a basically good person"

I'm beginning to think that people draw the wrong conclusions from Jesus's ministry.

Maybe it's because the Gospels put such an emphasis on Jesus "hanging out" with the social outcasts (the tax collectors, the sinners, the drunkards, etc.) and denouncing the upper-crust folks (the scribes and Pharisees) for their hypocrisy ("speaking truth to power," as we would say nowadays).

Perhaps that gives the false impression that all the people in between these extremes (the good ol' unassuming, salt-of-the-earth shopkeepers and tentmakers just plugging their way through life) were under Jesus's radar and not the target of His message.

If you look at the multitudes of people who flocked to hear Jesus speak or the diverse social strata that made up the first Christian converts, it's obvious that Jesus' message was vital for **everyone**.

To be sure, even though society is drawn to the anti-heroes and "bad boys," the world desperately **needs** more "basically good people." We need people who pay their bills

Yes, Your Butt STILL BELONGS IN CHURCH

on time, pay their taxes, say "please" and "thank you," hold open doors for strangers, throw their litter in the garbage can instead of on the sidewalk, use their automotive turn signal, adopt stray animals, play their TV and stereo at a decent volume so they don't disturb their neighbors, join service organizations, etc.

On the other hand, is being "basically good" **enough** to be found acceptable on Judgment Day?

After all, in Romans 3:23, Paul wrote, "For all have sinned and fall short of the glory of God."

In Jeremiah 17:9, the prophet declares, "The heart is deceitful above all things, and desperately wicked; who can know it?"

In Matthew 7:48 Jesus teaches, "Be perfect as your father in heaven is perfect." One can be **socially acceptable** by memorizing an etiquette guide, the driver's manual, or a rulebook of parliamentary procedure, but to be perfect requires a close relationship with Jesus Christ.

In Matthew 16:24-26, Jesus commanded His disciples to "follow me." While we can learn much about navigating life from other sources, Jesus did not command, "Follow *What to Expect When You're Expecting* or "Follow your inspirational desk calendar." He said, "Follow me."

"Basically good" people may respond to a compliment by diverting credit to a grandparent or their first-grade teacher, but in Colossians 3:17 Paul teaches, "And whatsoever ye do in word or deed, do all in the name of the Lord Jesus, giving thanks to God and the Father by Him." If you put your shopping cart back in the rack or hand out full-size candy bars at Halloween, people may eulogize you as "a good guy" and may even dedicate a bridge to you; but that's the totality of your reward. If your deeds were done

Yes, Your Butt STILL BELONGS IN CHURCH

for self-aggrandizement or just out of habit, they won't count on Judgment Day.

We judge ourselves by some self-serving standards of good citizenship, but Jesus upped the ante. In the Sermon on the Mount (Matthew 5), He declared that someone being angry with a brother without cause is in danger of the judgment just like someone who actually committed murder, and that whoever looks on a woman to lust after her has already committed adultery in his heart!

Seriously, with so many ways to mess up, how can anyone attain salvation just by watching socially conscious cartoons or attending a "woke" seminar? We need Jesus.

Even kind-hearted individuals who perform public acts such as offering rides to hitch-hikers or reminding everyone "if you can't say something nice about somebody, don't say anything at all" would get a creepy feeling if other people could **read their minds**.

Any sane person (no matter how well-respected by the community) would feel terribly **violated** if their friends and neighbors could read all the **secrets** God had written down about them – unless Jesus **blots out** those entries.

Functioning as a "basically good person" is a great starting point; but it is not an invitation to rest on your laurels.

To be pleasing to God, you need to be baptized and continue in a close walk with Jesus.

Yes, Your Butt STILL BELONGS IN CHURCH

Excuse 18:

"But I shouldn't have to obey the rules"

We humans love to fuss about rules, regulations, fine print, and deadlines.

We often declare them to be arbitrary, illogical, stupid, or unfair.

But mature adults recognize the **reality** of rules. Love 'em or hate 'em, we acknowledge that they exist and realize we have an uphill battle getting an exception made for ourselves.

Even if you're a cultured individual such as the conductor of the local symphony orchestra, that one time you show up at a classy eatery sans shoes and shirt, you're probably not gaining admittance.

Even if you're momma's favorite child, the carnival (to cover its own rear) is going to enforce that "You must be this tall for this ride" sign.

Even if you always pay your bills on time and only missed it this time because you stopped to let a bunch of ducklings

Yes, Your Butt STILL BELONGS IN CHURCH

waddle across the street with their mother, you'll still be assessed a late fee.

Even if you're the Employee of the Month, if you miss around and miss the "open enrollment" period for benefits changes, you'll have to wait until next year to sign up for dental insurance.

Even if you're volunteering for humanitarian endeavors such as Doctors Without Borders, if you refuse to divest yourself of pocketknives, box cutters, screwdrivers, etc. at the airport, you're not getting on the plane.

Even if you're an honors student, if you mess around and fail to get a parental permission slip signed, you'll be staying at school while everyone else goes on a field trip.

Being a person of class, culture, wealth, intelligence, or good moral character is not always enough to get you what you want in life.

Whether you're an atheist, a Buddhist, a Wiccan, or something else, certainly God wants your time on earth to be spent being kind and considerate.

But to enjoy the fulness of His blessings, He also wants you to become a Christian and **act** like a Christian.

And part of acting like a Christian involves associating with and working with other Christians.

I can find no instance of Jesus calling villagers to repentance and saying, "Oh, no, not **you** there in the back – you're good enough already."

I can find no instance of the apostles slapping Christians on the back and assuring them that associating with other Christians is "going way above and beyond the call of duty."

Yes, Your Butt STILL BELONGS IN CHURCH

You may squirm and fidget and offer counterproposals, but "them's the rules."

And no one has more authority and more power for enforcing rules than God.

Excuse 19:
"I'm too far gone to save"

Yes, this is the **flip side** of being "a basically good person" and not having to obey the rules.

"Aw, preacher, I **know** I'm going to hell."

There's no telling how many times those words have been spoken, with the same finality as "I just realized my daughter's school pageant was at 7:00 tonight and it's already 8:30! Oh, well."

If you want to have "Satan laughing with delight," give him a person on one of the extremes of the emotional chart.

So far, we've dealt mostly with the people who are too proud, haughty, and rebellious to submit to God's wishes. But Satan also works with people who feel worthless, alone, and hopeless.

Maybe they were browbeaten by their parents or a teacher. Maybe friends and lovers abandoned them. Maybe they've been the notorious "talk of the town" for far too long. Maybe they've been subjected to one "fire and brimstone" sermon too many.

Yes, Your Butt STILL BELONGS IN CHURCH

However they've arrived at their situation in life, they are dejected and begin to doubt God's ability and desire to make a new person of them.

Yes, Satan loves working with people who have these extreme views of their spiritual worth and opportunities.

He must work a lot harder with people who have a more clear-minded, level-headed perception of themselves and God.

Yes, these people understand that humans have prejudices, weaknesses, lusts, cravings, and a default mode of following the easier path.

They also understand that they are made in the image of God, that they are made a little lower than the angels, that God formed them in the womb, that the hairs of their head are numbered, and that God sent His Son to die for them.

They know that will stumble and fall often, but that they can pick themselves up, dust themselves off, and keep on trying to be faithful until death.

These people pose a challenge to Satan, and with enough study, prayer, and Christian fellowship, they can pose an **insurmountable** challenge to the Prince of Darkness.

The Bible is full of people who could have given up on having a right relationship with God.

Jonah boarded a ship with the ridiculous aim of getting as far away from God as possible, but God still had a mission for him. (The entire heavily populated Assyrian city of Nineveh was slated for destruction by God, but Jonah's preaching brought the entire population to repentance.)

King David was considered "a man after God's own heart," even though he essentially had a loyal soldier murdered to cover up an affair with the soldier's wife, Bathsheba.

Yes, Your Butt STILL BELONGS IN CHURCH

Even atheists can't escape the iconic (if unscriptural) image of Saint Peter standing at the gate of heaven acting as a desk clerk. But Peter was the apostle who "wept bitterly" after realizing that he had thrice denied having any connection with Jesus.

Most of us would take it for granted that if anyone is going to be in heaven, it would be Saint Paul. But Paul —always mindful of how he had rounded up Christians for execution before his conversion — had this to say in 1 Timothy 1:15: "This is a faithful saying and worthy of all acceptation, that Christ Jesus came into the world to save sinners; of whom I am chief."

The Old Testament writers were primarily interested in the nation of Israel, but many of their assurances are just as applicable to Christians.

For instance, Psalm 86:5 promises, "For thou, Lord, art good, and ready to forgive; and plenteous in mercy unto all them that call upon thee."

Micah 7:19 says, "He will turn again, he will have compassion upon us; he will subdue our iniquities; and thou wilt cast all their sins into the depths of the sea."

Back to the New Testament. In First John 1:9 we read, "If we confess our sins, he is faithful and just to forgive us our sins, and to cleanse us from all unrighteousness."

2 Peter 3:9 has been the basis for many a sermon: "The Lord is not slack concerning his promise, as some men count slackness; but is longsuffering to us-ward, not willing that any should perish, but that all should come to repentance."

Acknowledging our sinful nature is the first step of getting into a right relationship with God; but we must also admit that a solution is **available** and **doable**.

Yes, Your Butt STILL BELONGS IN CHURCH

Again, we're back to the extremes of the spectrum. Some people think they're flawless and God's gift to mankind. Others, while examining themselves "warts and all," see **only** the warts and forget about the "and all" that is pleasing to God.

Any good preacher – any good **Christian** – should be willing and able to let a fallen brother unload on him. But the "shoulder to cry on" needn't feel compelled to pry all the sordid details out of him. Yes, people have neglected their children, stolen their best friend's spouse, squandered a fortune on cocaine. Other people have done as bad or worse – and **still received forgiveness.**

"Aw, preacher, I know I'm going to hell" is a phrase the devil loves, loves, loves. Because the words are spoken without a full appreciation for what they entail. It's like a fresh-faced military enlistee blithely assuring his fiancée, "Yeah, I know war can be dangerous." That does not mean he is psychologically prepared to endure torture in a P.O.W. camp, watch his best buddy get his brains blown out, or kill another man with his bare hands.

Sure, church skits about promiscuous teenagers dying in a car wreck and going to hell are corny; but the fact remains that hell is not something to accept lightly.

I've watched TV dramas that portray hell as basically a gloomy neighborhood that has endured decades of urban blight. Such a portrayal is not pleasant, but it's not all that different from the reality that billions of people have learned to put up with on Earth. Just as our minds can't comprehend all the wonders of heaven, I think Hollywood is sugar-coating the horrors of damnation.

Did you study Dylan Thomas's poem *Do Not Go Gentle into That Good Night* in school? It deals in a generalized manner with shuffling off this mortal coil. The advice should be much more **emphatic** when dealing specifically with **eternal punishment.**

Hell is not something to accept with a sigh, a shrug, and a sense of resignation.

God instilled a **survival instinct** in each of us. It makes us wary of oncoming trains and feisty mountain lions, but we should also employ it in spiritual matters.

Whether you're a "basically good" person or a miserable wretch, fight tooth and nail to avoid eternal punishment.

Because Satan wouldn't want it that way.

Yes, Your Butt **STILL BELONGS IN CHURCH**

Excuse 20:
"My family wasn't very religious"

I feel **blessed** that my parents always saw to it that my brother and I made it to church.

(My father was also an elder and an adult Bible class teacher at the time of his death.)

At this phase of my life, it is pointless to conjecture on when and **if** I would have become a Christian without that upbringing. I might sigh, "I really dodged a bullet there," but I keep on facing the world.

So, I can feel your pain if you grew up in a family that placed little or no importance on religious observance.

But that was then; this is **now**. As the popular saying goes, "Today is the first day of the rest of your life." (I first heard this phrase in a long-ago commercial for Total cereal, but the *Washington Post* attributes it to Charles Dederich, the founder of Synanon, a self-help community for drug abusers and alcoholics.)

There is no denying that the first 18 or so years of your life have a massive impact on your personality, habits, prejudices, and ambitions. Whether you are told things explicitly ("Early to bed and early to rise...") or absorb

Yes, Your Butt STILL BELONGS IN CHURCH

values through observing your parents' example, there are a million and one predispositions you pick up.

But people **do change** as they enter the dating game, make new friends, further their education, launch a career, move to another city, etc.

Some families have absolutely no qualms about wearing the same clothing for three days in a row and bathing only on Saturday night. But if you are smitten with a beautiful girl who digs your sense of humor and your cleft chin but **balks at your body odor**, you may very well learn new hygiene habits.

Maybe your childhood diet consisted entirely of good ol' Southern working-class beans-and-taters. With enough cajoling, your college classmates could very well introduce you to Thai, Greek, or French cuisine.

Perhaps you were raised in a racist family, but if your son or daughter presents you with that first biracial grandchild, your heart is likely to melt and your attitudes soften.

People who never dreamed they could have more than a high school diploma or a G.E.D. attend college in their 30s, 40s, 50s, and beyond.

People enter adulthood with very strong attitudes about work ethic, sports teams, etiquette, politics, money management, and leisure activities – but your in-laws, co-workers, or club members could very well make you do a 180-degree turn. ("I always made fun of the eggheads who listened to classical music, but it's really pretty cool when you give it a chance.")

For good or ill, normal, healthy individuals can and do change over time.

Don't get me wrong. I don't **envy** people who have wasted decades without God and Christ. They have a lot of ground

Yes, Your Butt STILL BELONGS IN CHURCH

to make up. But neither do I wring my hands in **despair**. There is still time to learn and grow – starting **now**.

"My family wasn't very religious" may be 100 % true, but don't use it as an excuse to limit your **future** options. (My brother and I like to make fun of our younger cousin for the circular reasoning of his finicky childhood protestation "I cannot eat that because I have never eaten it **before**.")

What's done is done. If you suffered the consequences of not knowing (a) your spouse's birthday, (b) the speed limit on a particular stretch of country road, or (c) the value of surge protectors, difficult passwords, and computer-file backups, don't cry over spilled milk. **Make use of your knowledge going forward.**

I pray that you will find support from Christians who are patient with your super-basic questions and your tottering baby steps; but those questions and those baby steps are central to your being pleasing to God.

Excuse 21:

"None of my friends go to church"

I decided at the last minute to cut this excuse a little extra slack.

That's because of a story by Nancy Keates on page A9 of the August 4, 2020 *Wall Street Journal*: "Why some teens ignore coronavirus restrictions."

Obviously, this article wasn't talking about obstacles to worship, but some of the scientific information is worth consideration when discussing why young people do things that older Christians find unfathomable.

According to Keates, a "neurological mandate" in the adolescent brain compels the typical young person to throw caution to the wind when socializing with peers.

Young adults tend to be tagged as irresponsible, but they are just "doin' what comes naturally" (to quote a song from the musical *Annie, Get Your Gun*).

Yes, Your Butt STILL BELONGS IN CHURCH

Maybe you dozed during that section of biology class, but it's well-known that the human brain isn't fully formed until around age 26. Many lifelong habits/abilities are set in stone by age six, but there is another "growth spurt" during the adolescent and emerging-adult stages.

During this phase, there is an impulse to break away from family and interact more with peers. Socializing and seeking new experiences is how young people forge their identities.

High dopamine levels support motivation and reward-driven learning, which steers young people toward novelty, thrills, peer approval, and immediate gratification over future gains. For people of any age, this can lead to risky decisions.

If you are a parent of a teen or adult child, you are probably painfully aware of this reality. You have probably also learned that scolding, lecturing, and ultimatum-delivering do little to solve the problem and may even be counterproductive. (Truth be told, your own parents – and **their** parents -- probably learned the same lesson. Did you ever know **anyone** who cheerfully accepted the "If all your friends were jumping off a bridge..." cliché without some smart-aleck comeback?)

I will deal with this topic again in one of my concluding chapters, but for now I would like to call for people of all ages to do some sensible **balancing**.

Yes, people need friends for normal social development and merging into the adult world, but there are friends and then there are **friends**.

When you start hanging out with people with shared interests (hobbies, sports, politics, etc.), it's statistically unlikely that you will wind up with a crew 100 percent made up of people who will choose knocking on doors and

Yes, Your Butt STILL BELONGS IN CHURCH

spreading the Gospel instead of rollerblading or getting a mani-pedi.

If you were raised in the church, some of the people you run with may not "get" the whole "Jesus thing" or be able to wrap their minds around church attendance. If your friends take a "live and let live" attitude, you can work with that.

On the other hand, if your friends constantly use the Lord's name in vain, spray-paint graffiti on church walls, and take a **perverse pride** in undermining your religious background, you have chosen (chosen!) the wrong group of "friends." They are **bullies** and a demonstrably bad influence on you.

Young people tend to have strong opinions about which sneaker brands are cool, which beer tastes nasty, and which vehicles are the ones to aspire to owning. If you can do Quality Control on **these** things, you can and should do Quality Control on your companions.

Despite what old folks might think, young people do not operate with a hive mentality like the Borg collective in the *Star Trek* universe. They have the ability and the freedom to make **choices**.

There is always a give and take among true friends. They may have to understand that you can't stay up all night because you have a big job interview tomorrow, or that you had to replace your car's engine and simply can't afford to go on that weekend trip. By the same token, true friends will understand that you can't join up with them until Sunday **afternoon**, or that you like to say a short prayer over your pizza.

Stand-up comedians and political pundits crave the "mic drop moment": a statement that is so dead-on, so incisive, so indisputable, so devastating that they can drop the microphone and leave that thought etched in your mind.

Yes, Your Butt STILL BELONGS IN CHURCH

"None of my friends go to church" is **not** a "mic drop moment" witticism. (Just as divulging "None of my friends get colonoscopies" or "None of my friends leave a tip" or "None of my friends report their under-the-table income" doesn't prove that those are **praiseworthy** attributes.)

It is a mere statement of fact and a **starting point** for what to do with that nugget of information.

Whether you are being pulled away from the church or whether you have never been a churchgoer, "None of my friends go to church (and they haven't been struck by lightning yet)" doesn't have to be a "case closed" declaration.

You have a choice of **settling** for that sad fact and letting your companions shackle your possibilities —openly mocking and subverting any spiritual inclinations you might have.

Or you can choose to widen your circle to include some people of faith, while **uplifting** the nonbelievers around you.

Yes, Your Butt STILL BELONGS IN CHURCH

Excuse 22:
"My spouse/kids/ parents get enough religion for all of us"

I am glad that my son completed two Red Cross swimming courses. Now I don't have to worry so much if he happens to be clumsy on a boat or riverbank. And I can live vicariously through his frolicking in a pool.

But even though I saw to it that he **got** to his swimming classes, I myself did not magically gain the ability to swim. I would still sink like a rock.

Let's talk about voting. If everyone else at your address goes to the polls and comes home with an "I Voted" sticker, but you **abstain** – and the referendum your whole family passionately wanted to pass fails by one vote, **it still fails by one vote.** The intentions you couldn't be bothered to act upon do not magically get retrofitted into the tally just because you share DNA or a marriage license with a voter.

If you wear yourself to a frazzle to make sure your family is well-fed but neglect your own nutritional needs, you will

Yes, Your Butt STILL BELONGS IN CHURCH

wind up deficient of protein, vitamins, minerals, or whatever. When elderly parents suffer chronic loss of appetite, their concerned children may try various ways to remedy the situation (easier-to-chew foods, liquid supplements, appetite-enhancer medication); but standing around saying, "Here, bask in my healthy glow" is not a viable option.

Are you starting to see a trend? A mere familial or fraternal connection to a Christian is no substitute for being an active Christian yourself.

Certainly, Christians are commanded to lead others to Christ, but we are not guaranteed a "plus one."

The controversial governmental policy of "chain migration" makes it easier for the aunts, uncles, cousins, and other relatives of immigrants to come to America; but scripture contains no example of "cutting the red tape" for relatives of Christians or "moving the relatives of Christians to the head of the line."

Many businesses host "Bring Your Children to Work" events. But there is no corresponding "Bring Your Family Members to Paradise" event.

When the Book of Life is opened on Judgment Day, there will be individual names listed – not **and associates**."

When Andrew (a disciple of John the Baptist and a future apostle) first heard Jesus preach, he didn't think "I can soak up enough religion for the whole extended family." He hurried to find his brother Simon Peter so he could listen as well. (John chapter 1.)

When Simon Peter baptized the Roman centurion Cornelius (Acts chapter 10), Cornelius's kinsmen and near friends were also baptized. There was no indication that Cornelius's mere presence could save them all.

Yes, Your Butt STILL BELONGS IN CHURCH

Read some histories of the early church when Christians largely met in the homes of other Christians. There are no accounts of a "designated worshipper" for the family shooing everyone else out of the house on the Lord's Day and saying, "Go out and have a fun day. I've got this."

It is amazing how some people can compartmentalize their interaction with their families. They love watching TV with them, eating out with them, going on vacation with them. But spend eternity in a perfect place with them? ("Meh.")

Yes, God's blessings may come to your household even if not everyone attends church. Your spouse and children may exhibit more generosity and self-control. Church members may bring meals when someone is sick, perform chores when someone is injured, provide job leads when a family member is unemployed.

But these are all earthly, temporary benefits. Your relatives and the church members **can't save your soul without your participation**. Even if Ancestry.com could show that every single one of your ancestors was a practicing Christian, the fate of your own soul is still in your hands.

Religious observance is fundamentally different than other areas of life where we look with bemusement on the activities of loved ones. You can make shake your head and chuckle when Dad refuses to wear a pink shirt, Mom fills every nook and cranny with Hummel figurines, or the kids listen to awful music. These are subjective choices that don't amount to a hill of beans in the Big Picture.

I know it's simplistic, but there's a lot of truth to the old saying "The family that prays together stays together."

If you are complacent about attending church with your family or if you think they are a bunch of idiots for wasting time and money on an imaginary white-bearded old man in the clouds, this is an issue that calls for soul-searching

Yes, Your Butt STILL BELONGS IN CHURCH

and deliberation. You are disrespecting them on a very basic level. Do not chip away at their commitment by making them envious of your free time.

It's just a higher level of questions like "Will we or will we not take out a life insurance policy? Will we or will we not send the kids to private school? Will we or will we not move across the country for a big job opportunity?" These are not areas where you can kick the can down the road or agree to disagree. They have major repercussions.

Not making a choice **is** making a choice.

If you don't mind that people may pity your family or that your family members suffer sleepless nights because of you, there is unquestionably something dysfunctional about your love for your family.

And church – not a recliner, not a bar stool -- is the best place to seek solutions.

Excuse 23:
"All they care about is your money"

When someone resorts to this not uncommon excuse, I start wondering who the nefarious "they" are.

Is the excuse-maker laser-focusing his ire on an inner circle of movers and shakers who are in love with filthy lucre, or does it apply to Christians in general? If the latter, I guess Joe Lapsed-Christian imagines all the other men, women, and children in the congregation hanging around after he leaves so they can divvy up his $20 bill.

That takes a special kind of paranoia.

Over the past few decades, the news media and TV dramas have done a good job of highlighting televangelist scandals. We've all seen narcissistic preachers who are either overpaid or embezzle church funds to pay for a lavish lifestyle of mansions, private planes, and mistresses.

I think those are the exceptions. Most church congregations have more modest funding. Some rural churches and inner-city churches are barely hanging on.

Yes, Your Butt STILL BELONGS IN CHURCH

The minister may get a meager stipend or members of the congregation may take turns delivering a sermon for free.

Especially in the internet era, operating a brick-and-mortar church seems a terribly **labor-intensive** way of conducting a scam. There are plenty of con games you can run from home, while wearing your sweatpants. So it seems like a stretch to stereotype all Christians and all congregations as being money-grubbing.

"All they care about is your money" is a knee-jerk response from someone who has let a bad experience (or imagined bad experience) sour him on the world.

To be sure, there are money-related issues plaguing churches. Some congregations (like some universities with their gargantuan endowments) accumulate too much money in the bank instead of finding good works in the community. Some preachers do soft-pedal certain sins rather than antagonize a prominent member who might leave or reduce his contributions.

But these are **side issues** from "All they care about is your money." These are things to roll up your sleeves and prayerfully address. They are not justification for **avoiding** church.

We certainly set different standards for people in **non-religious** fields. Most of us probably have a favorite hairdresser, barista, grocery clerk, insurance agent, accountant, and mechanic. These are people who greet us with a big smile, engage in chitchat, and ask how our family members are doing.

But...we try to erase the reality that a business relationship is our main tie to these people.

They have employers and families to think about. If we switch hairdressers, accountants, etc. but frequently drop in to gab with the old one, no matter how nice and genuine

Yes, Your Butt STILL BELONGS IN CHURCH

they are, we will soon discover that most of their smiles and chitchat are understandably reserved for their remaining **paying customers**.

We might quibble over inflation and surcharges, but most us of don't begrudge a hairdresser, mechanic, etc. being paid for their services. And we understand that our "friendship" suffers if there is no longer a business relationship.

Ah, but church is different. Even if we're financially well off, we think we should be able to sit there in the air-conditioned sanctuary, enjoy the music, and contribute next to nothing to the upkeep of the building or the mission work.

Hmm…seems all **we** care about is our money!

Try for a better attitude. In the late 90s I was abruptly downsized out of a good-paying job and had to settle for a job that paid a lot less. (No kidding—I cried when I heard how **much** less.) But I kept my chin up because of series of books that were quite inexpensive; every hour I sweated, I knew I was making almost enough to buy one of those books.

So take pleasure in thinking about how your contribution will buy construction paper for a young Sunday School pupil, provide meals for the homeless, or build a new church building in Central America.

The more time you spend **being** a cheerful giver, the less time you'll have for negativity.

Yes, Your Butt STILL BELONGS IN CHURCH

Excuse 24:
"Church? That's not how I roll!"

A self-absorbed world has placed the flippant observation "That's not how I roll" on a pedestal.

Whether it's a matter of wearing a safety belt, observing etiquette guidelines, practicing safe sex, or obeying the rules of fair competition, people **worship** the idea of "That's not how I roll."

There is no denying that people are different. Each person has his own personality, background, tastes, quirks, priorities, strengths, weaknesses, talents, and goals.

To a certain extent, I can appreciate the candor of people who are upfront about their likely (mis)behavior; but it does not merit an automatic commendation ("You go, girl!" or "That's my boy!"). Sometimes it's just **sad**.

Wide-open exhortations of "Follow your bliss," "Be true to yourself," "Think outside the box," and "March to the beat of a different drummer" **may** lead people to new horizons and praise-worthy accomplishments; but without the right moral compass, those sentiments will more likely lead to catastrophic wrong turns.

Yes, Your Butt STILL BELONGS IN CHURCH

Not all "rolls" are created equal. History is filled with people who "did it my way," but those people are not interchangeable. Consider Gen. George Custer, Saddam Hussein, TV's Fred Rogers, Adolf Hitler, Genghis Khan, Teddy Roosevelt, Mother Teresa, Bonnie and Clyde, Harriet Tubman, Charles Manson, Billy Graham, Sen. Joseph McCarthy, Joseph Stalin, Susan B. Anthony, Babe Ruth, and Thomas Edison. Some would be placed in the "saintly" column by historians; some would be cast as deplorables; some would have a more mixed legacy. But, obviously, "that's the way I roll" does not create a level playing field.

Family background, geography, and socioeconomic status do not necessarily lock us into a lifelong way of rolling.

You may bear a physical resemblance to your father and share a love of baseball with your father, but you are not a **clone** of your father. Your mother's genes and lessons, your experiences in school and the workplace, and the choices you make in life will all contribute to your individuality.

Perhaps everyone in your small hometown waves a Confederate flag, eats mainly "beans and taters," and listens to the Grand Ole Opry every Saturday night. For good or ill, as you explore more of the world, you may tuck your flag away, learn to enjoy French escargot, and spend a fortune on jazz or classical records.

If you grew up poor, you may continue your frugal ways up to the point of insisting on a plain pine box for your funeral, even if you're a billionaire. Or if you finally achieve a six-figure income, you may automatically go on a spending spree and dive deep into debt. Your way of rolling is subject to change.

The success of support groups shows that "the way I roll" is not an immutable characteristic.

Yes, Your Butt STILL BELONGS IN CHURCH

For an addictive personality, wallowing in alcoholism or drug abuse comes naturally. For people with a certain temperament, the natural response to frustrations is physical violence. With rows and rows of junk food in grocery stores, why **wouldn't** you stuff your face? When you lose a spouse or a child, **of course** you want to sink into depression for the rest of your life. In certain situations, who **wouldn't** want to kill themselves?

But therapists, support groups, and "12-steps" programs **do** help people suppress or change the way they roll. People learn to resist the temptation to use drugs and alcohol to solve their problems. People in anger-management courses learn more socially acceptable means of conflict resolution. People learn portion control and positive self-image. People learn to look on the positive side of life and dispel suicidal thoughts.

Believe it or not, God does not pre-program or hardwire any of us to be adamantly opposed to salvation. As James the brother of Jesus (or the **cousin** of Jesus, as Catholic theology teaches) tells us in James 1:3, "Let no man say when he is tempted, 'I am tempted by God'; for God cannot be tempted with evil, neither tempteth He any man."

Our way of rolling is neither a blessing nor a curse; it is just a **snapshot** of where we happen to be at any given moment.

Simply put, if you are rolling in a direction that takes you away from church membership or participation, it is because you **choose** to have priorities, habits, and companions that facilitate that situation.

A swaggering gait and a declaration of "That's not how I roll" do not act as a magic talisman. They will not prevent you from being slandered, sued, or assaulted by a lover you've wronged. They will not prevent you from being fired for insubordination. They will not prevent you from

Yes, Your Butt STILL BELONGS IN CHURCH

undergoing costly dental procedures when you refuse to floss. They will not keep you from being visited by the IRS when you play fast and loose with your deductions.

And they will not protect you from eternal damnation.

At the risk of sounding blasphemous, I sometimes like to imagine the late comedian Richard Pryor portraying God in a Judgment Day sketch.

"Say **what**? After the way you lived, you expect to roll on through the Pearly Gates like nothin' never happened? Like H you will! I'll tell you what you need to do, boy – you can just roll yo' (rear end) on down to the lake of fire!"

Don't be the punchline of a Richard Pryor routine. Before it's too late, start rolling in the right direction.

Excuse 25:
"There's too much doctrine"

I am fascinated by people who profess to have an unerring knack for knowing when there is too much doctrine in church.

Is this an innate ability like perfect pitch or fast metabolism?

Is it something you must train for and be certified for, like passing the bar exam or completing a medical internship?

Is there something like a litmus strip or a metal detector that helps you identify an overabundance of doctrine?

Inquiring minds want to know.

Of course, I'm being facetious. When people say, "There's too much doctrine," they're really saying, "Speaking for **myself**, there's too much doctrine."

But even with that clarification, I still feel compelled to probe further.

Human beings tend to underestimate themselves and seek the path of least resistance.

Yes, Your Butt STILL BELONGS IN CHURCH

"The heck with the coach. I simply can't do another pushup or lap."

"Another 15 minutes of piano practice? Noooooooo!"

"My eyes will explode if I read another chapter of my history assignment before I revert to couch potato mode and play my video games."

"Yes, my 401(k) retirement account would be much larger if I could contribute just five dollars a day more, but I'll **die** without my morning cup of espresso."

For our own good, we need parents, teachers, supervisors, life coaches, 12-steps groups, and others to push us beyond our self-imposed limits.

Maybe we do it grudgingly, but in most aspects of life, we eventually embrace the concept of "No pain, no gain."

But for some church-resistant people, doctrine gets placed in a whole different category. It is viewed as **unimaginably more demanding** than wind sprints or making the perfect souffle or mastering a complex dance routine.

I won't lie to you. It is **possible** for religious bodies to accumulate too many bells and whistles. On October 31, 1517, Martin Luther launched the Protestant Reformation by posting 95 theses criticizing beliefs and commandments that the Roman Catholic Church had developed over the course of a millennium and a half. The Puritans, as well as the Restoration Movement of the early 1800s, proclaimed that even the mainstream Protestant denominations were clinging to too many superfluous or wrongheaded ideas.

But some people (like the Princess in the story *The Princess and the Pea*) are so hyper-sensitive that they can't tolerate **any** doctrine.

Yes, Your Butt STILL BELONGS IN CHURCH

Be honest. Strip away the Jewish dietary and ceremonial requirements that are no longer binding on Christians, and the Bible is mostly narratives, poetry, prophecy, and commonsense advice for moral living.

The essential instructions for how one becomes a Christian, how church leadership is to be arranged, and how one continues along the Christian pathway are **remarkably compact**.

In Matthew 11:29-30, Jesus assured his followers, "Take my yoke upon you, and learn of me; for I am meek and lowly in heart: and ye shall find rest unto your souls. For my yoke is easy, and my burden is light."

Again, some religious bodies may place unreasonable burdens on you, but in its purest form, Christianity most definitely **doesn't** demand tons of memorization or force you to walk a tightrope in a hurricane.

If someone chafes at the bare-bones requirements of Christianity, it is probably because a specific "thou shalt not" hits them where they live ("What's a little adultery among friends? What happens in Vegas stays in Vegas") or because they have a generalized chip-on-the-shoulder resistance to authority. ("Hmph! Ain't no cop, no spouse, no inspector, no teacher gonna tell **me** how to run my life.")

Neither of these knee-jerk responses are anything to be proud of.

Doctrine is not something optional. Paul advised Titus (Titus 2:1) "But speak though the things which become sound doctrine."

Doctrine is important both for uplifting the spirits of Christians and for defending Christianity against its many opponents. "Holding fast the faithful word as he hath been taught, that he may be able by sound doctrine both to exhort and to convince the gainsayers" (Titus 1:9).

Doctrine is God's way of providing us a valuable tool, not His way of grinding us under His heel. "All scripture [is] given by inspiration of God, and [is] profitable for doctrine, for reproof, for correction, for instruction in righteousness that the man of God may be perfect, thoroughly furnished unto all good works." (2 Timothy 3:16-17).

(Where else are you going to get instruction in righteousness in the modern world: *People Magazine*? *Cosmopolitan*? *The Jerry Springer Show*?)

I know humans like to drive around aimlessly without stopping to ask for directions. They like to plunge into the assembly of a swing set without reading the instructions first.

But such actions seldom turn out well.

With the Bible, to avoid problems down the road (problems much more serious than winding up in the middle of a cornfield or having three bolts left over), sometimes you have to put on your big boy (big girl) underwear, quit your bellyaching, and read the instructions.

Yes, Your Butt STILL BELONGS IN CHURCH

Excuse 26:
"Church is so boring"

There is no denying that the church experience can sometimes be yawn-producing.

This is especially true of congregations where members deliver passionless, assembly-line prayers, where ministers have a sing-song delivery of their sermons (think of the teacher played by Ben Stein in the TV show *The Wonder Years*), where Bible classes consist of a lecture with no give-and-take, where the auditorium's acoustics are so terrible that they suck all the emotion out of every word spoken in them.

Different temperaments and different learning styles can contribute to the feeling that church is boring.

In a later chapter, I will deal with how church leadership can make improvements.

In the meantime, I want to focus on the people who are doing the complaining – and challenge their contentions.

For one thing, why pick on religion when you're generalizing about boredom?

Yes, Your Butt STILL BELONGS IN CHURCH

Although not everyone is "into" automobiles with the same fervor, I never hear people say, "**Cars** are so boring." True, manufacturers may get in a rut of playing it safe by giving their main makes nearly indistinguishable body styles, and motorists may yearn for the past or dream of the future; but they still don't say, "Cars are so boring."

People may switch to bicycles or mass transit because of maintenance expense or carbon footprints, but people simply don't declare that "Cars are so boring." They may have to research foreign sports cars or hang out with classic car enthusiasts (lovers of cars with tailfins, running boards, rumble seats and other aspects that add "character"), but they don't write off all cars.

Similarly, I never hear people say, "**Food** is boring." They may lament the frequency of leftovers at home, whine about the blandness of food in the school cafeteria, or protest the lack of variety in local restaurants in their small town; but they don't give up on food as a whole. (I am writing about normal, healthy people here. Senior citizens with poorly functioning taste buds may sigh, "Nothing tastes appetizing anymore," but that is a problem with the eater not the fare.) No, they find a brand, dish, or eatery that **does** titillate their palate.

Although individual clergymen or congregations may have a pizazz deficiency, church is **not** inherently boring. Its sacred text, the Bible, contains accounts of love, hatred, friendship, betrayal, jealousy, rivalry, war, sacrifice, deception, migrations, quests, infertility, false imprisonment, crime, punishment, repentance, and much more.

Don't get me started on the miracles; if you can get excited about a video of a **skiing squirrel**, you can get excited about floods destroying all of humanity except eight souls, fire and brimstone destroying Sodom and Gomorrah, Moses parting the Red Sea, prophet Jonah being preserved

Yes, Your Butt STILL BELONGS IN CHURCH

in the belly of a great fish for three days, a crowd of 5,000-plus being fed with five loaves of bread and two fishes, the blind and lame being cured, and all the rest.

If sex and violence are what you crave in movies, novels, and video games, the Bible has sex and violence aplenty – with **constructive lessons** to draw from the incidents.

Humans never tire of asking the Big Questions, such as "Why am I here?," "What is the meaning of life?," and "Is there more to existence than what I'm seeing?" The Bible/church deals with those questions (or should), so how can it possibly be boring?

Things become boring when they are viewed as irrelevant to one's daily life or long-term goals ("When will I ever use calculus after school? Will my job interview for a dental hygienist position **really** involve knowing *Romeo and Juliet* inside and out?")

Things become boring when they are too abstract to create any emotional involvement. Think about being cornered by a long-winded acquaintance who goes on and on about people you've never met and probably never will meet. ("So, anyway, my cousin Mikey's brother-in-law's piano teacher...")

Although holy scripture doesn't use specific modern terms such as "internet troll," "Covid-19," "downsizing," "soccer mom," "bucket list," or "Tide Pods," I can't think of any broad theme of modern life that is **not** covered by the Bible. ("There is nothing new under the sun," as Solomon wrote in Ecclesiastes 1:9.)

The Bible can tell how to respect your parents and how to deal with rebellious children. It extols the qualities to look for in a mate. It tells how to interact with neighbors, both good and bad. It tells how to handle yourself at work. It tells what you do and do not owe the civil government. It tells how to handle the emotional highs and lows of life. It tells us how to prioritize and how to deal with the temptations that are common to humanity.

As I said, I will eventually get around to discussing how church leaders can make worship more engaging; but for right now, I want non-attendees to look at themselves in the mirror and ask, "Am I part of the problem? Could I work on my short attention span and my unreasonable expectations?"

Instead of feeling sorry for yourself because of the torture chamber that is church, just be glad that God isn't bored with **you**. Rejoice that the omnipotent being who created the stars and the mountains and the great whales cared enough about you to send His only begotten Son to die for you – and still has big plans for you.

Yes, Your Butt STILL BELONGS IN CHURCH

Excuse 27:
"I'll wing it"

I shudder to think how many people meander through life with an arrogant attitude of "I'll live my life as I see fit, and then if it turns out that there **is** an afterlife...well, I'm pretty fast thinking on my feet and I'll figure something out."

Yes, in our own nearsighted way, we're always granting **superhuman status** to ourselves or someone we admire, because of our perceived notions of cleverness, toughness, or invincibility.

Beware: our false bravado and our little conceits aren't doing us any favors.

Sometimes it's a winking admiration for a friend. ("Ol' Mike is such a slick-tongued devil, he could've stabbed Fred Rogers on Main Street and talked the prosecutors into giving him Manhattan Island and the keys to Fort Knox.")

Sometimes we're doting on our children or grandchildren. ("Little Johnny is so bright at three years old, I just know that by the time he's in high school he will have cured the common cold and invented a time machine.")

Sometimes we exhibit grudging admiration for people we don't necessarily like. ("My mother-in-law is so tough,

Yes, Your Butt STILL BELONGS IN CHURCH

she'd have those MS-13 criminal gangs squalling for mercy.")

But what if all this hyperbole meets up with reality?

If Ol' Mike had really killed the avuncular kiddie show host, he would most likely be put **under** the jail and achieve the sort of infamy reserved for John Wilkes Booth and Lee Harvey Oswald.

Little Johnny may very well turn out to be valedictorian and win a scholarship (if he doesn't level off and become a slacker), but the odds are against him Changing the World. (Even Bill Gates and Jeff Bezos have been unable to cure the common cold or invent a time machine.)

Your mother-in-law may be the proverbial battle-ax, but if she crossed MS-13, she would most likely wind up raped, riddled with bullets, beheaded, and thrown in a ditch.

"Glory days" are not a reliable predictor of future performance. Quarterbacks and school bullies can get cancer, diabetes, and ALS just like the rest of us. Rich guys with a fleet of sports cars still wind up penniless, because of bad investments, the obsolescence of their business, or some betrayal. Beauty queens, TV stars, and rising politicians can all die in plane crashes.

I don't like the insurance industry term "acts of God" to describe natural disasters, but just for the sake of argument, let's pit acts of God against attributes of man.

Charm, good looks, and glibness all pale beside tornadoes, hurricanes, tidal waves, earthquakes, volcanic eruptions, and wildfires.

It takes an amazing amount of hubris to think that we can pull an improv act and undo a lifetime of disobedience. It takes an unbelievable amount of gall to think we can fritter

Yes, Your Butt STILL BELONGS IN CHURCH

away our lives, reject Christ, and then make excuses on Judgment Day.

Romans 14: 11, 12 tells us "For it is written, As I live, saith the Lord, every knee shall bow to me, and every tongue shall confess to God. So then every one of us shall give account of himself to God."

That's scripture, the inspired word of God.

What exactly is the basis for any thoughts to the contrary?

"Um, uh, my overactive imagination?"

Case closed.

Yes, Your Butt STILL BELONGS IN CHURCH

Excuse 28:
"My God wouldn't be such a hardnose"

"A hilarious exposé of the absurdities inflicted upon Hollywood's creative community by meddling film and TV executives."

That's how Amazon describes Leonard B. Stern's book *A Martian Wouldn't Say That!*

At the core of this collection of memos written by various television network executives is a memo written to the writers of the TV series *My Favorite Martian*. (The show ran from September 29, 1963 to May 1, 1966 on CBS. It starred Ray Walston as extraterrestrial Uncle Martin and Bill Bixby as Tim O'Hara.) The memo reads, "Please change the dialogue on page 14 – a Martian wouldn't say that."

Pause for a second and digest that bit of unsolicited advice.

An executive, seeking to micro-manage and justify his hefty paycheck, came out and declared definitively, "A Martian wouldn't say that!"

Yes, Your Butt STILL BELONGS IN CHURCH

First, we don't even know that Martians exist. (There's way less evidence for Martians than for the existence of a Supreme Being.) Even with all the UFO sightings, books about ancient aliens, and breathless speculation about the possibility of microbes eking out an existence on Mars, there is nothing tying intelligent life specifically to the red planet.

Second, it follows logically that the executive had never *met* a single Martian on which to base his assumption.

Third, the executive had certainly never met *all* the Martian race.

Fourth, even if the executive had experienced the privilege of shaking hands (tentacles?) with every single Martian, that would not make him an expert on all their longings, ambitions, deepest secrets, personality quirks, or reactions under pressure.

So, you can see why the audacity of that executive would inspire Stern to start collecting such examples of know-it-all meddling.

When it comes to religious matters, many of us are just as pompous and tone-deaf as that executive.

We declare, "A loving God wouldn't condemn someone for (fill-in-the-blank)" or "**My** God wouldn't mind if I worshipped him in such and such a fashion."

True, it is permissible —even admirable – to speak of "my God" (in a reverent sense, not the ubiquitous exclamation "OMG!") We should feel that God loves us and cares for us. We should feel that He knew us from the womb, has the hairs of our heads counted, and sent His only begotten Son to die for our sins. We should feel that part of the Trinity (the Holy Spirit) has been sent to be a Comforter to Christians.

Yes, Your Butt STILL BELONGS IN CHURCH

He **is** "my God" in the sense that He is the only true deity, the only Creator of all that exists, the only safe haven in time of danger.

We should put Jehovah him above all other gods (whether idolatrous images or material wealth). There should not be a single friend, relative, or business associate driving a wedge between us.

But a dismaying number of Christians, lapsed Christians, and Never Christians who place a decidedly **possessive** slant on the phrase "my God."

To them, God is Alexa, Siri, or a genie – a wish fulfiller at their beck and call. They want to relegate the Supreme Being to serving as a trained monkey. He is treated as an ever-handy rubber stamp, an alibi, a co-conspirator. We feel we can put words in His mouth with impunity.

Such people brag, "Me and God or me and Jesus are **just like that**" (imagine me twisting my middle and index fingers together).

Wow. I have so many questions for people who know Jesus so intimately. How tall was He? What was his affectionate name for Joseph? Who was his favorite sibling? Can you rank all the apostles by how much he liked them? What was his favorite dessert? His favorite season? His preferred sleeping position? Was he a morning person? Did he ever whistle or hum? Did he have any allergies? What exactly did He write in the dirt when a mob wanted to stone the woman who was caught in adultery?

What? You haven't the foggiest notion how to answer any of these questions? Maybe you should stop spouting off as if you and Jesus finish each other's sentences.

Some people have no qualms when it comes to pontificating about what "an all-loving God" would or wouldn't do. ("An all-loving God wouldn't care if my cousin

Yes, Your Butt STILL BELONGS IN CHURCH

had consensual sexual relations with goats. An all-loving God wouldn't care if I missed church 50 weeks out of 52.")

I'm not sure where this confidence originates.

Is it like the old defensive-about-charges-of-racism response ("Hey, some of my **best friends** are all-loving gods")? Do you have a **doctorate** in all-loving gods? Did you serve an **internship** as a clerk for a bunch of all-loving gods?

I am jealous of the people who have a special insight into the comings and goings of an all-loving god.

All **my** information about **the** all-loving God comes from the Bible. He is indeed loving, but He also demands purity and justice.

The God of the Bible is not the namby-pamby, vacillating milquetoast of a pushover whom some people make Him out to be.

He stripped physical immortality from mankind, banished Adam and Eve from the garden, sent Cain away for killing his brother, wiped out all but eight humans with the Flood, confused the languages of the people who built the Tower of Babel, destroyed Sodom and Gomorrah, turned Lot's wife into a pillar of salt, unleashed 10 plagues on Egypt, forced the Israelites to wander in the wilderness for 40 years because of their unbelief, blocked Moses from entering the Promised Land because of a momentary indiscretion, wrenched the throne away from Saul because of his disobedience, punished David for his sin with Bathsheba, sent the 10 northern tribes into Assyrian captivity, sent the southern tribes into Babylonian captivity, etc.

Some scholars try to paint "the God of the New Testament" as meeker and milder than "the God of the Old Testament, "; but their case is weak. In the New Testament, God

Yes, Your Butt STILL BELONGS IN CHURCH

allowed Judas to commit suicide. An angel caused Herod Agrippa I to be eaten of worms when he accepted adulation as a god (Acts chapter 12). Ananias and Sapphira (Acts, chapter 5) were struck dead when they lied about a donation they made to the church. 1 Corinthians 6:9-10 lists unrighteous people who will not inherit the kingdom of God. The Revelation does not deal gingerly with the majority of the 7 churches of Asia Minor.

God made man in His image, but some people are determined to make God in **their** image. To them, every single "thou shalt" and "thou shalt not" **matching their personal behavior** is spot-on brilliant! Everything that **aggravates their conscience** is something to be **ignored or explained away**. What a coincidence! I mean, what are the odds??? (Slim to none, I would say.)

How does our unqualified confidence work in other aspects of life?

We might assume, "My husband would never look at another woman" or "My wife wouldn't mind if I brought three buddies home for supper unannounced" or "My daughter would never fool around" or "My son would never drink alcohol" or "My business partner would never utter a racial slur" or "My investment counselor would never betray my trust" or "My senator would never compromise on that piece of legislation."

But only God is omniscient.

We may have a good **general grasp** of the character and integrity of the people in our lives, but we simply cannot know what they would do in a moment of weakness.

Take an honest look around you and at the world at large.

You'll find a never-ending stream of surprises, disappointments, miscalculations, and scandals. Long-held secret grudges bubble to the surface. Heart-rending

Yes, Your Butt STILL BELONGS IN CHURCH

admissions of "I just don't love you anymore" burst forth. Political dynasties are toppled by unforeseen scandals. Strange bedfellows forge political alliances. Unkind words erupt from the most unlikely of sources. Momentary lapses of judgment ruin reputations.

If you can't be 100 % certain how people you've shared a marital bed with, eaten barbecue with, or studied from the beginnings of their public life will react in a given situation, how in the world can you put words in the mouth of the deity who created the entire universe? How can you **contradict** what the Supreme Being has preserved in writing for us?

People who try to dilute or pervert what God says are in denial. They are false teachers and false prophets. We are to be the light of the world, but they are pulling excuses from whence the sun don't shine.

In Titus 1:15-16, Paul declared, "Unto the pure all things are pure: but unto them that are defiled and unbelieving is nothing pure; but even their mind and conscience is defiled. They profess that they know God; but in works they deny him, being abominable, and disobedient, and unto every good work reprobate."

The amount of chutzpah it requires to **sanctify** what God has **condemned** is mind-blowing.

The TV executive who blurted out a silly statement about Martians will be anonymously immortalized as a buffoon as long as a certain book is in circulation. The Christian who makes excuses for himself and acts as an enabler for others is in danger of **eternal** consequences.

Excuse 29:
"Church and my job don't mesh"

Good, honest work has always been important to God.

He gave Adam and Eve responsibility for tending the trees in the Garden of Eden.

The Old Testament contains lessons such as the one in Proverbs 13:4: "The soul of the sluggard desireth, and hath nothing; but the soul of the diligent shall be made fat."

God chose Joseph, a carpenter, to be the earthly father of Jesus. Lowly shepherds were the first humans to announce the birth of the Christ child. Jesus taught parables about laborers.

Paul supported his preaching by working as a tentmaker, so that no one could say his ministry was just a "get rich quick" scheme.

In Second Thessalonians 3:10, Paul told the Thessalonians "For even when we were with you, this we commanded you, that if any would not work, neither should he eat."

So, no, work commitments are not an afterthought that God didn't really consider when setting up the church. He just doesn't mean for work to be an **obstacle** to worship.

Yes, Your Butt STILL BELONGS IN CHURCH

Work-related objections to attending church seem to run in three categories: (1) conflicting schedules, (2) uneasiness in the workplace, and (3) total incompatibility between one's worship and employment.

"I have to work during church time" has many parallels to "Sunday is my one day a week to sleep in." Neither excuse should be taken lightly.

Work and church bumping up against each other? Been there, done that. My high school job in a convenience market required me to work every Saturday and Sunday, alternating between an evening shift and a morning shift. When my missing services every other Sunday morning became an issue, my parents got us back into the habit of attending Sunday **evening** services as well. (We had drifted away from that when we moved 10 miles farther from the church building.)

More recently, the retailer where I work was open from 1:00-5:00 p.m. on Sundays for a span of more than a decade. Thankfully, employees rotated the Sundays, but it still meant years of rushing out the church door before the closing hymn, gobbling down a fast-food lunch (we love our buffets!), and rushing to make it back to evening services. But I made a point of **making it work**.

Depending on their job skills and the employment situation in their community, some people **don't** have a lot of choices about their work schedule. For others, it **is** a choice (or at least a rut that developed from choices made long ago). They **like** getting 40 hours pay for working three 12-hour weekend shifts. Or they like not having so many bosses around. Or they like having weekdays wide open for running errands.

These preferences are understandable, but they should not be so ingrained that they drive a permanent wedge between you and the church.

Yes, Your Butt STILL BELONGS IN CHURCH

We **need** police officers, nurses, doctors, and utility repairmen available during church hours, but those individuals don't have to be **you** – at least not on a long-term basis.

If work is constantly preventing you from attending worship services, you don't have to deliver an ultimatum to the boss; but you need to start brainstorming a schedule more conducive to worship.

Perhaps you need to change shifts or take a different position with the company. Whatever, if you're **complacent** about the dilemma, it is unlikely to improve on its own.

As for being ribbed, joshed, hazed, razzed, ostracized, and marginalized at work…

First, take a deep breath and make sure you're not the victim of **thin skin** and an **overactive imagination**.

Are you the only person at work who has a nickname and gets teased? Or does the gang also tease people who are bald, overweight, wear mismatched clothing, act henpecked, support the "wrong" sports team, drive the "wrong" brand of car, brown-bag it instead of eating at a fancy restaurant, etc.?

Could there be other reasons that you are avoided at the water cooler or lunch table? Do you have body odor, tell the same old uninteresting stories over and over, and try to sell school candy to your co-workers?

If you can truthfully say that you are being picked on or passed over for plum assignments solely because of your Christianity, then you need to talk to your boss or the Human Resources Department.

Allowing this toxic environment to persist is not good for you, the company, or anyone.

Yes, Your Butt STILL BELONGS IN CHURCH

If you go all the way to the top and your concerns are laughed off, you need to stand up for yourself – and Christ.

Finally, let's address the issue of jobs that just do not mesh with Christianity.

Some jobs are in a gray area – what I would call sin-adjacent. For instance, a stand-up comedian who is clean-living but whose manager has him performing in decidedly seedy venues. Or a monogamous actor who must play **characters** who are sexually promiscuous. You'll have to wrestle with your own conscience about whether you are serving or harming the cause of Christ in such cases.

Other occupations are more clear-cut. If your job requires you to get clients sloppy drunk, procure underage sex partners for rock stars, send out phishing emails to steal innocent people's personal financial information, run a protection racket for the mob, peddle illegal drugs, etc., you definitely need to make some hard decisions.

I think that everyone would agree that one would be a **hypocrite** if they held such jobs but pretended to be a God-fearing Christian.

Unfortunately, most people in these situations take the easy way out: instead of giving up their **jobs**, they just give up going to church. Hypocrisy problem solved! (Or so they think.)

In whatever way your job drives you away from God, I implore you to change your ways.

Matthew 16:26 asks two of the most important rhetorical questions in history: "For what is a man profited, if he shall gain the whole world, and lose his own soul? or what shall a man give in exchange for his soul?"

Money, prestige, and power won't mean a thing on Judgment Day.

Yes, Your Butt STILL BELONGS IN CHURCH

If your job is really standing between you and Christ, choose Christ.

Best-case scenario for doing otherwise: your job supports your lavish lifestyle and pays you a pension until you croak – and then you have only suffering and remorse for the **rest of eternity**.

Believe me, having been downsized a time or two, I understand why people cling to jobs. I know that good-paying jobs are not "a dime a dozen."

But I also know that people all over the world quit good jobs every day, often with little regret.

I'm not talking just about hotheads, lazy bums, and people who recognize the level of their incompetence.

There are **successful**, highly respected people who surprise their peers by asking for a demotion, jumping to a competitor, or changing careers entirely. Maybe they want to spend more time with their families. Maybe they no longer feel challenged. Maybe they're no longer proud of the product or service the company provides. But they take risks and many never look back.

I know it's not **easy** to give up a "safe" job, but it's demonstrably **doable**.

And just how "safe" is a job that puts you in danger of hellfire?

Yes, Your Butt STILL BELONGS IN CHURCH

Excuse 30:
"God and I grew apart"

Small wonder that people embrace this excuse.

In olden times, a marriage ended either because of death, infidelity, or severe abuse. We've now become accustomed to "no-fault" divorce. We grudgingly accept that slowly, gradually – imperceptibly at first – couples sometimes drift apart.

Because of health issues, friendships, co-workers, and other factors, marriage partners develop different needs, values, interests, and goals. Romantic love fades away and they eventually decide they would be better off alone or with other partners.

We also know about drifting apart from our experiences with classmates. Think of all the idealistic, naïve, short-sighted yearbook pronouncements of "Best friends forever." True, some friendships stay strong all the way from preschool until death; but most don't.

Pie-in-the-sky expectations may be 100 percent sincere and no one is really the villain, but the dynamic changes.

Classmates leave town, further their education (perhaps switching majors multiple times), start a demanding

Yes, Your Butt STILL BELONGS IN CHURCH

career, and discover new hobbies. Their circle begins to include spouses, in-laws, children, and grandchildren.

The former best buds may exchange long Christmas cards and may share uproarious anecdotes when they finally meet up again at the 25-year class reunion, but they are different people than when they were 18. They'll insist they need to stay in closer touch, but probably won't see each other again until the 30th reunion.

So...drifting apart is normal and acceptable.

But wait...it doesn't work that way with you and God.

In Malachi 3:6, God the Father declares, "For I am the Lord. I change not."

Hebrews 13:8 describes the Son as "Jesus Christ, the same yesterday, and today, and forever."

Yes, people may wax and wane in their fervor, respect, and (perceived) need for God. This is because they **choose to ignore** the warning signs of drifting away. They choose to spend less and less time with God's people and God's word. They choose to pay more attention to worldly messages. They choose to respond to the siren song of the lust of the eye, the lust of the flesh, and the pride of life.

They may describe it as **growing** away from God, but it really means **shrinking** our possibilities and the richness of our blessings.

During all this, God is immutable. He still loves us and His expectations of us remain the same. We may anger Him and disappoint him, but He does not grow bored or distracted.

God continues to want the best for you, just as Jesus described himself as a mother hen yearning to shield Jerusalem beneath his wings. (Matthew 23:37)

Yes, Your Butt STILL BELONGS IN CHURCH

The rift between humans and God does not have to be **permanent**. Yes, the longer you stay away from God, the harder it is to overcome inertia and restore the former relationship; but the reward is worth the effort many times over.

Yes, Your Butt STILL BELONGS IN CHURCH

Excuse 31:
"I've got faith; I don't need works"

Raising the issue of "faith and works" is like opening a can of worms – a can of worms that could grow to fill a bookshelf.

But I think scholars have gone too far in exaggerating a supposed conflict between the teachings of New Testament authors Paul and James.

Paul, appropriately enough, **dealt in good faith** when extolling the virtues of faith. He may have anticipated –but didn't condone – the watered-down mockery of faith that would develop.

If you want a simplified examination of the interplay of faith and works, let's look at the example of a set of parents who rear a son whose upbringing is particularly labor-intensive, either because of physical disabilities (autism, muscular dystrophy, blindness, etc.) or delinquency (drug abuse, brawling, grand theft auto, etc.). He'll require at least 18 years of hard work and sleepless nights; he might even be in his thirties when he ventures out on his own.

Yes, Your Butt STILL BELONGS IN CHURCH

An accountant could crunch the numbers and determine that the son literally couldn't ever repay his parents for everything they've done.

But in a healthy family, there would be no scorekeeping. The parents could still be happy, proud, and satisfied.

That's because they'll judge their child by the fruits of his attitude, priorities, and character.

If he becomes a contributing member of society, loves his own wife and children, keeps an open mind to sage advice from mom and dad, and treasures parental visits and phone calls, they can rest easy. Even if they're not a mushy family that vocalizes "I love you" with every other breath, his actions will show that the parents are loved, respected, and appreciated.

On the other hand, if he does the exact opposite of everything his parents advise, constantly bails on family dinners at the last minute, mistreats his wife and children, curses his parents, breaks promises to run errands for them, ignores birthdays and anniversaries, and always displays a "What have you done for me lately?" demeanor, no matter how many times he mumbles, "I love you," the parents' love will be tested and their hearts broken.

They **will** be enumerating and regretting the sacrifices they made for him. The concept of "tough love" will pop up. They will be less forthcoming with bailouts. They will finally start playing favorites among him and his siblings. They may even cut him completely out of the inheritance.

No matter how loudly he protests, his actions will speak louder than words when it comes to how he truly regards his parents.

Like good human parents, God doesn't have a points system. where you gain so many points toward an afterlife in heaven by (a) attending Sunday morning worship, (b)

Yes, Your Butt STILL BELONGS IN CHURCH

showing up for midweek services, (c) bringing brownies to the bake sale, and (d) saying "Bless you" when someone sneezes.

Like good human parents, God does judge by the heart (and the actions and inactions propelled by the heart).

Many lapsed Christians hide behind their faith, but it is usually a **dead faith**.

Seriously, if you show up at church only for weddings and funerals, let your Bible gather dust, and avoid "fuddy-duddy" Christian acquaintances when you spot them in the mall, why should God feel happy, proud, and satisfied about you?

How does such a weak faith demonstrate your **fear** of God? Your **reverence** for God? Your **gratitude** for God?

This is not a deep and abiding faith, but the sort of distracted answer one gives a survey taker. ("Faith? Yeah, I heard something somewhere about 'Jesus saves' one time. Put me down for some of that!")

God encompasses an infinite amount of forgiveness, but that forgiveness presupposes the recipients acknowledging that they **need** forgiveness. God is constantly pleading, "Give me something to work with."

You may have unflappable faith in the financial stability and honest dealings of Prudential Insurance, but if you don't care enough to pay premiums and file claims, that faith will be for nothing.

You may have faith that your trusty Mustang will get you to the other side of the country, but if you're too lazy to get off the sofa, fuel up the vehicle, and head out, you're not going to be reaching the other side of the country.

Is it unreasonable for God to expect a little sincerity, enthusiasm, and "get up and go" out of you?

Yes, Your Butt STILL BELONGS IN CHURCH

If you have faith in a new stock offering – if you feel in your heart of hearts that it is going to skyrocket – you will probably scrape together every dime you possess and urge your broker to invest it. If you have faith in the weatherman – if you believe deep down that a tornado is really going to rip through your neighborhood – you will take evasive action. If you have faith that Jesus Christ died to wash away your sins, you will ...mutter, "Yeah, keep me on the membership list."

What is wrong with this picture???

Rest assured, you can have the utmost faith in God's **truthfulness** and **power** in delivering on his promises of blessings; but one should have an equal amount of faith that a just God will feel obligated to **enforce the strings attached to those blessings.**

Faith doesn't have to mean self-flagellation and vows of poverty, but it should involve **something** more than lip service – or it means nothing at all.

Don't let a corrupt definition of faith and its benefits cause you to be blindsided on Judgment Day.

Yes, Your Butt STILL BELONGS IN CHURCH

Excuse 32:
"If only I had a sign..."

Some people insist that if God would just get down off His high horse and deign to send them a miraculous sign (Niagara Falls running uphill? a tree stump turning into a mighty oak? their late grandfather's image appearing in the swimming pool? a winged angel fluttering down the street?), they would **gladly** believe in Jesus and check out this "church" thingy.

They think this a more-than-reasonable request, but it goes against the idea of walking by **faith**. It implies that the allmighty God **owes** us more than He has already delivered (the resurrection of Jesus and the accounts of it).

"Seeing is believing," these people insist; but that is not necessarily true. "People believe what they want to believe" is a frequent comment by someone who attends my church, and it may be closer to the truth.

Let's be honest; people who **demand** a sign are probably going to keep changing the goalposts for what constitutes proof of the existence of God and the importance of Jesus. The sign must match their preconceived notions and not interrupt their status quo, or they would write it off as a

Yes, Your Butt STILL BELONGS IN CHURCH

David Copperfield magic trick, an amazing coincidence, a hallucination, or an optical illusion.

Seeing is believing? The Bible freely admits that some of the Jews who heard Jesus preaching and saw him performing miracles did not believe. Judas traveled with Jesus, ate with Jesus, saw Jesus control the elements – but he betrayed him and committed suicide rather than repent in a Godly manner. Peter's faith wavered when he walked on water and when he denied Christ three times. After the resurrection, the Jewish leaders attributed Jesus's feats to the power of Satan and made excuses for the empty tomb. Christians remained a minority in the first century no matter **what** miraculous gifts were given to some of them.

Yes, when Jesus was conducting his earthly ministry (false messiahs were a dime a dozen at that time) and when the apostles were spreading the news of the resurrected Christ, there was a **need** for miraculous healings and other manifestations of the Holy Spirit in order to break through the clutter and attest to the authority of the speakers. (Even "Doubting" Thomas had to feel Jesus's wounds to overcome his skepticism.) **Now** we have those lessons preserved for us in a book that has withstood centuries of scrutiny.

The Bible and people whose lives have been changed by Christ are here as a resource – just as we can learn lessons from Holocaust survivors and *The Diary of Anne Frank*, without having to crank up Holocaust gas chambers and take them on tour.

We should be cautious of nuclear war based on the reports of survivors of Hiroshima or Nagasaki (and the G.I.s who surveyed the devastation). We shouldn't **need** a nuke exploded in a different town every week just to **update** and **personalize** the message.

Yes, Your Butt STILL BELONGS IN CHURCH

Even if one can admit **intellectually** that God exists, that Jesus is His Son, that Jesus died and was resurrected…there is another hurdle to jump **emotionally**.

How do you know that seeing God or Jesus or angels face-to-face would be a true, meaningful, long-term **gamechanger** for you?

Yes, some people respond readily when they see something in black and white or hold a piece of evidence; but in this world of cynicism, conspiracy theories, and hidden agendas, many do not.

No matter how often anti-vaxxer arguments are debunked, some people still refuse to get vaccinated.

No matter how many videos or artifacts we display, some people still think the Apollo 11 moon landing was "filmed out in the desert somewhere."

No matter how much evidence is presented for the spherical nature of the earth, flat-earthers double-down on their beliefs.

Voters will cling to one candidate or party no matter how much dirt is unearthed by multiple sources.

Patients can **nod** and mutter "Uh huh" when the third doctor they've sought a diagnosis from shows them the same lab results and insists, "Those cigarettes are going to kill you" or "You have to drop 50 pounds to prevent a heart attack" – but unless the information "hits them where they live," they will have a hard time changing their habits.

You may tell yourself that if God would just quit being obstinate and appear to you in a vision, you would be a rip-roaring Good News spreader – a "be there twice every Sunday, knock on every door" Christian; but now it's **my** turn to be skeptical.

Yes, Your Butt STILL BELONGS IN CHURCH

If studying the Bible and getting to know good Christians personally hasn't changed you yet, I have my doubts about the impact of a burning bush or a talking donkey.

In Jesus's parable of the rich man and Lazarus (Luke 16:19-31), while in Hades, the rich man begged that Abraham would send Lazarus back to the land of the living to warn the rich man's five brothers to change their evil ways and not end up in torment. Abraham bluntly replied that if the brothers would not heed Moses and the prophets, they would not believe **even if one returned from the dead**.

If you admit that Jesus was at least "a good man" and "a wise teacher," accept that blunt statement.

We have already been given our sign: like Jonah emerging from the great fish, Jesus arose the third day, triumphing over death and offering salvation to all those who will believe.

Stop making excuses. Humble yourself and make an honest effort to learn from the Bible and those who are already faithful Christians.

Use some common sense. You don't need a time-traveler to dump January snow on your carpet on Labor Day to know that **winter follows autumn**. And you don't need a modern parting of the Red Sea to know that Judgment Day follows this life.

Excuse 33:
"Hey, I send in my donations"

I have learned that some Christians feel satisfied to sit at home and send a check to the church.

There is never a shortage of uses for money (keeping the utilities paid, maintaining the church bus, advertising, soup kitchens, paying for radio broadcasts, etc.), so bless you for doing at least that much.

But you are **cheating** yourself if that is the totality of your church involvement.

There are different levels of enjoyment from giving. I always get a warm, fuzzy feeling when I drop money into a Salvation Army kettle. But I felt even better years ago when my parents and I went to the basement of a local variety store and helped parcel out Christmas gifts for needy families. (The floor was sectioned off for the families, with notes such as "Five-year-old girl, eight-year-old blind boy…") And I have no doubt I would have felt even **more** connected if we had participated in **delivering** the gifts and meeting the recipients face to face.

Yes, you can pat yourself on the back and say, "My generous check will pay for new cushions for **whoever** is

Yes, Your Butt STILL BELONGS IN CHURCH

sitting on the front pew these days." But it would be so much more rewarding to **meet** (or become reacquainted with) that front-pew occupier!

Even if you receive a quarterly financial statement, donating from afar does not give you a good view of how the money is spent or how the church is doing.

If you attend regularly, you might find you need to voice an opinion that replacing the frayed carpet is more urgent than the plans to buy new stained-glass windows. You might decide that "Yes, this sounds like a good mission, but this other country sounds like a more fertile field." You might learn that the fill-in preacher really deserves to be called upon more often.

You limit your options and tie one hand behind your back when you donate remotely.

You can let the status quo glide along, gradually phase out your participation, or let problems fester until you have an ugly blow-up.

If you **accompany** your money to worship service, you can monitor problems and opportunities on a week-by-week basis.

Nowadays we demand transparency and accountability from our government agencies and financial institutions. Sadly, some of us settle for no transparency and accountability from church.

Become fully involved.

Yes, Your Butt STILL BELONGS IN CHURCH

Excuse 34:
"Hey, I'm willing to settle"

Society has a strange love-hate relationship with overachievers.

Sometimes when people excel in their field (sports, entertainment, business), we sign onto their social media platforms by the hundreds of millions, grab their (ghost-written) books, and name streets after them.

Other times, we bring up the old "All work and no play makes Jack a dull boy" maxim and dismiss them as a showoff, a goody two-shoes, a know-it-all, a teacher's pet, or a brownnoser. When they "give 110 percent," we accuse them of "running up the score" in an unsportsmanlike manner.

Perhaps it is this latter view of achievement that gives some people an excuse for **slacking off** in their relationship with God.

"I'm not greedy," they might say. "I'll be happy with the humblest cottage in heaven. I don't need to rack up a bunch of extra points."

Judgment Day in the Bible is described as a **pass-fail** test. It is extremely foolhardy to convince yourself that you

Yes, Your Butt STILL BELONGS IN CHURCH

know **exactly** how little effort to put into entering heaven by the skin of your teeth. It's dangerous to declare, "That's enough reading the Bible! I've prayed more than my share! Who cares if there are still strangers who need a little kindness?"

You get **one shot** at Judgment Day, unlike many earthly endeavors.

If you put a pinch too little salt in your grandmother's recipe, well, you'll know better the next time.

If you make a D on your first test in Dr. Hinkley's class because you didn't bother to go over your notes a second time, well, you have a chance to pull your semester grade up by rectifying the oversight on the **next** test.

If you make a bad first impression on your spouse's aunt because you didn't bother to learn the taboo topics, you can work up a game plan and strive to charm her the next time.

Judgment Day does not allow such "do-overs."

Part of the problem is that people who want to coast into heaven with the least amount of effort are living in a **bubble**. They are convinced theirs is a brilliant plan that will leave them precious time for hobbies **and** shield them from being labeled a "Jesus freak."

One of the key elements to success is being able to recognize when you are **failing**.

If you are trying to develop a plant-based meat substitute that 9 out of 10 people will accept, and 5 out of 10 people **reject** it, you **know** you need to go back to the drawing board.

If your garage band is trying to create a Top 10 Hit and it doesn't even crack the Billboard Top 100, you **know** you'll have to try again.

Yes, Your Butt STILL BELONGS IN CHURCH

If you're racing to develop a vaccine for a new virus and it's effective in only a handful of patients, you **know** your team will have to regroup and take a different approach.

Success in one's relationship with God can be trickier.

If you're trying to succeed with minimal effort, you won't know if you made it until it's **too late**.

If you're bebopping along thinking everything is okay, it's a situation as melancholy as Paul Simon's 1975 song *Slip Sliding Away:* "You know the nearer your destination, the more you're slip slidin' away."

If you're trying to make it into heaven without breaking a sweat (and "trying" may be an overly generous term, since heaven is just an **afterthought** for most of the people I'm describing, as in "Heaven? Oh, uh...don't bug me. I got that covered. The tortoise and the hare, man"), you are probably already living in a fool's paradise.

There is nothing wrong with having humble tastes and settling for achievable goals. You don't **have** to be super-ambitious about material things. In 1 Timothy 6:6-8, Paul said, "But godliness with contentment is great gain. For we brought nothing into this world, and it is certain we can carry nothing out. And having food and raiment (clothing) let us be therewith content." But the contentment involves the amount of our earthly treasures, **not** skimping on the amount of **godliness** in our lives!

You can't deny that lack of commitment and enthusiasm has **consequences** in the physical world. If you hate the rat race and have been satisfied to be a humble mailroom clerk for the past 40 years, fine; but if the new boss repeatedly catches you "watching the clock," don't expect him to do you any favors and find you another position if the mailroom is phased out. If your spouse must constantly

Yes, Your Butt STILL BELONGS IN CHURCH

nag you to get you to perform even **half** your share of the chores, don't expect a harmonious household.

Serving God doesn't have to mean fretting, anxiety, and insomnia. A puppy-dog-like dose of **enthusiasm** will do the trick. ("Oh, boy – I've been blessed with another day! What can I do to please God today?")

Maybe you have an uncanny knack for guessing how many jellybeans are in a jar or which racehorse will suddenly pull ahead in the final stretch. **Maybe** you think that talent will translate into an infallible guide for knowing how little you can do and still be pleasing to God.

But I wouldn't count on it. That is one monumental **gamble**. That constitutes tempting God. ("I **dare** you to toss out a good customer who shows up every Christmas and Easter!")

God loves **win-win** situations. It makes **Him** happy when humans know the joy of serving His Son.

But if your lackadaisical lifestyle makes it come down to a **win-lose** situation, **you** will be on the losing side.

Yes, Your Butt STILL BELONGS IN CHURCH

Excuse 35:
"I've paid my dues"

Far too many lapsed Christians like to treat their past experiences as a lifetime **inoculation** that requires no booster shots.

If at any point in their lives they have been immersed, sprinkled, invited to come down the aisle at a tent revival, or enticed to lay their hand on the radio during a sermon, they think they've gone above and beyond the call of duty.

Whether you phrase the philosophy as "Once saved, always saved" or something else, it was a **heresy** when the apostles were establishing the church, and it has not gotten any better with age.

I know there are influential religious leaders who will cherry-pick certain verses and twist doctrines completely out of context, but they are giving a false sense of hope when they do so.

When the Holy Spirit instructed the apostles in what to preach or what to write, He did not fill every verse with a comprehensive rehashing of everything that pertained to "faith" or "grace." He did not expect people to apply loose, self-serving definitions to "believe" or "obedience" or

Yes, Your Butt STILL BELONGS IN CHURCH

"forgiveness." He expected people to make a **good-faith effort** to use the commonsense God gave them and view doctrine in a larger context.

The Bible abounds with scripture that demolishes the "once saved, always saved" interpretation

In 1 Corinthians 9:27, Paul wrote, "But I keep under my body, and bring it into subjection; lest that by any means, when I have preached to others, I myself should be a castaway." Yes, even Paul – who worked as a tentmaker to support his preaching and went to his death for the cause of Christ – realized he could still throw away his salvation if he became complacent.

In 1 Timothy 4:1, Paul warned the young evangelist, "Now the Spirit speaketh expressly, that in the latter times some shall depart from the faith, giving heed to seducing spirits, and doctrines of devils." Yes, it is possible to depart from the faith.

In James 5:19-20, James (a half-brother of the Lord and a pillar of the church in Jerusalem) advised, "Brethren, if any of you do err from the truth, and one convert him; Let him know, that he which converteth the sinner from the error of his way shall save a soul from death, and shall hide a multitude of sins." Yes, erring from the truth puts Christian's souls in danger!

Peter delivers a stern warning in 2 Peter 2:20-21: "For if after they have escaped the pollutions of the world through the knowledge of the Lord and Saviour Jesus Christ, they are again entangled therein, and overcome, the latter end is worse with them than the beginning. For it had been better for them not to have known the way of righteousness, than, after they have known it, to turn from the holy commandment delivered unto them." Not a lot of wiggle room.

Yes, Your Butt STILL BELONGS IN CHURCH

The writer of Hebrews (some say it was Paul, others disagree) wrote in Hebrews 3:12-14, "Take heed, brethren, lest there be in any of you an evil heart of unbelief, in departing from the living God. But exhort one another daily, while it is called today; lest any of you be hardened through the deceitfulness of sin. For we are made partakers of Christ if we hold the beginning of our confidence steadfast unto the end." Steadfast unto the end. That sounds nothing like "Self-identify as a Christian and then coast for the rest of your life."

In 1 John 2:24-25, John wrote, "Therefore let that abide in you which you heard from the beginning. If what you heard from the beginning abides in you, you also will abide in the Son and in the Father. And this is the promise that He has promised us – eternal life." So eternal life is connected to "abiding," not just a casual, long-ago encounter.

In Colossians 1:21-23, Paul wrote, "And you, that were sometime alienated and enemies in your mind by wicked works, yet now hath he reconciled in the body of his flesh through death, to present you holy and unblameable and unreprovable in his sight: If ye continue in the faith grounded and settled, and be not moved away from the hope of the gospel, which ye have heard and which was preached to every creature which is under heaven; whereof I Paul am made a minister." Continue. Grounded. Settled, Not moved. That doesn't sound like impulsively rushing to the baptistry with a bunch of teenage buddies and later neglecting the church. Living a hedonistic lifestyle doesn't exactly jibe with being "holy and unblameable and unreprovable."

"Take heed unto thyself, and unto the doctrine; continue in them; for in doing this thou shalt both save thyself, and them that hear thee," advised Paul in 1 Timothy 4:16. If a one-time confession of Christ is sufficient, why would one need to "heed" and "continue"?

Yes, Your Butt STILL BELONGS IN CHURCH

John 5:24 quotes Jesus as proclaiming, "Verily, verily, I say unto you, He that heareth my word, and believeth on him that sent me, hath everlasting life, and shall not come into condemnation; but is passed from death unto life." I am not a scholar of ancient manuscripts, but I learned that the Greek tense used in this scripture does **not** indicate a "one and done" situation. The "hearing" and "believing" (**really** believing) are **ongoing processes**.

Jude (another half-brother of Jesus) tells us in verses 20 and 21 of his one-chapter epistle, "But ye, beloved, building up yourselves on your most holy faith, praying in the Holy Ghost, Keep yourselves in the love of God, looking for the mercy of our Lord Jesus Christ unto eternal life." We must actively **keep** ourselves in the love of God. We are supposed to **build** upon our faith.

In Revelation 2:10 the brethren at Smyrna were told, "be thou faithful unto death, and I will give thee a crown of life." Faithful unto death. That is not the same as tagging along to Easter service with your spouse five—no, I think it was seven—years ago.

The writer of Hebrews says in chapter 4, verse 11, "Let us labour therefore to enter into the rest, lest any man fall after the same example of unbelief." We don't **earn** salvation through works, but work is expected of us.

In 1 Corinthians 10:12, Paul wrote, "Wherefore let him that thinketh he standeth take heed lest he fall." That doesn't leave much room for our cockiness and arrogance.

Cynical times make even pure-hearted people watch out for fine print and disclaimers and exclusions. But when it comes to salvation, no matter how many times we see the word "if" in the Bible, we see salvation as completely **without conditions**.

Yes, Your Butt STILL BELONGS IN CHURCH

Proponents of "once saved, always saved" sometimes snort and dismiss some reprobate with the statement that, "Hmph! He wasn't **really saved** to start with."

That is a presumptuous retroactive claim to being able to read the heart of another person.

Let's use the example of a civic-minded reformer who decides to run for governor. He (or she) takes out a huge loan to fund 50 percent of the campaign himself. He spends long hours with experts on health, education, and transportation, hammering out an achievable platform. He tirelessly crisscrosses the state, shaking every hand and kissing every baby. He never turns down a chance for an interview or a debate. He persists in the face of every scurrilous lie propagated by the opposition.

But then overpowering unforeseen circumstances arise. He learns that his next-biggest donor is expecting all sorts of corrupt favors. An anonymous caller makes a credible threat against the lives of his spouse and children. Try as he might, he never rises above 20 percent in any of the reputable polls.

Finally, the candidate tearfully drops out of the race.

Is it remotely fair to say, "Ah, he wasn't really committed to being governor to start with"?

Life is full of things that challenge our active participation in church. Some people prayed for the first time in years after the terrorist attacks of 9-11; others were totally disillusioned by the senseless destruction. Sometimes change is more gradual; hang around bad companions long enough and they'll rub off on you, weakening your commitment to Christ.

But whether one's distancing from religion is abrupt or gradual, there is no scriptural or logical basis for

Yes, Your Butt STILL BELONGS IN CHURCH

automatically assuming either (a) He wasn't saved to start with or (b) he's saved no matter what.

Just because a lie has been around for a while, it doesn't make it any less a lie. Don't lean on "once saved, always saved" and expect it to save you when your religious observance is infrequent or nonexistent.

Excuse 36:
"But what if…"

One of the highlights of my elementary school years was the arrival of *My Weekly Reader*, a slender periodical featuring short stories, activities, and timely news briefs about topics such as Britain's royal family or the Los Angeles smog.

My Weekly Reader had a summer edition, and one issue contained a short story that really speaks to the "But what if…" mentality.

After more than 50 years the title and the plot details elude me, but I'll try to get at the gist of the narrative.

The residents of a quaint little town are going about their regular Tuesday (?) activities when – for a reason I can't remember – one of the townsfolk has a crisis of confidence. "How do we know it's Tuesday? Maybe the calendar maker was wrong and it's really **Wednesday**?" The doubt spreads like a virus. Soon everyone else in town is deciding that maybe it's really Thursday or Saturday or (in the case of the minister ringing the church bell) Sunday.

In this comedy of errors, the town descends into chaos, until common sense prevails.

The abandonment of common sense goes hand in hand with the "what if?" excuse.

Yes, Your Butt STILL BELONGS IN CHURCH

"What if some scribe made a 'typo' and scripture was changed from its original meaning of 'For heaven's sake, **don't** gather in my name'?"

"What if we're all just part of the Matrix?"

"What if Jesus was really an extraterrestrial who dropped by the earth, yanked the chain of some superstitious Jews, and has no intentions of ever coming back?"

"What if the apostles concocted an elaborate hoax about the resurrection but then had a collective brain fart, forgot it was a hoax, and gladly suffered martyrdom for something they had known wasn't true?"

Um, in tinfoil-hat conspiracy theory circles, these remotely possible arguments might gain some traction, but let's apply the brakes (and some logic).

Let's say you're sending your kids for a sleepover. A **responsible** parent would have a checklist that included sending toiletries and a change of clothing, making sure the hosts don't leave firearms lying around, and communicating which snacks might trigger severe allergic reactions.

A **paranoid** parent would lose sleep over questions such as "What if little Johnny's parents are in the Federal Witness Protection Program and the Mafia tracks them down and burns down the house? What if a giant sinkhole swallows the house? What if they're really vampires?"

Are such far-out concerns legitimate reasons for spoiling a childhood rite of passage?

Donald Rumsfeld (who served as secretary of defense under presidents Gerald Ford and George W. Bush) famously observed, "You go to war with the army you have, not the army you might want or wish to have at a later time."

Yes, Your Butt STILL BELONGS IN CHURCH

This fits in with the people who invite paralysis through an endless stream of "What if…" and "Maybe…" Sure, it would be ideal if we could pore over mint-condition handwritten originals of the Gospels, ask Siri-like questions of a visible, winged angel, manifest the Holy Spirit by shooting sparks from our fingers, and chat with Jesus as He tops off a glass of water-turned-into-wine; but that is not the hand we have been dealt when dealing with matters of faith.

People harbor some honest, sincere questions about the Bible; but many conjectures have the stench of desperation about them. People embarrass themselves by scrambling for loopholes, throwing everything against the wall to see what sticks, and doing everything possible to keep from confronting the truth.

God's grace is mind-blowingly vast, but the plan of salvation doesn't have to be perplexing. As Saint Paul wrote in First Corinthians 14:33, "For God is not the author of confusion, but of peace, as in all the churches of the saints." Confusion comes from willful resistance to God's plan.

People who dedicate their lives to being active Christians are making a leap of faith, but it does not have to be a **blind** faith. Armed with the Bible and a good selection of apologetics books, you can be **reasonably** sure that God exists, that He sent His Son to live as a human and die for our sins, that Jesus was resurrected, that Jesus is preparing a dwelling place for his followers, and that those followers need to be both talking the talk and walking the walk while they await Christ's return.

Not making a choice…is a choice in itself.

Dithering, handwringing, procrastinating, and vacillating may come naturally to some people, but such "neutrality" comes with **consequences**.

Yes, Your Butt STILL BELONGS IN CHURCH

If you can't decide which products to put in the Amazon shopping cart, which delivery address to use, or which method of payment to use...guess what? You're not receiving a package from Amazon!

If you conjure up unending objections to every college you consider, every insurance policy you consider, and every combo meal you're offered, you will miss out on college, go without insurance, and stay hungry.

When it comes to religion, there is no safety in straddling the fence.

As Bob Dylan sang, "It may be the devil or it may be the Lord, but you're gonna have to serve somebody."

Throw away your wild theories and choose to serve the Lord.

Excuse 37:
"I'm entitled to my loopholes"

We fuss about judgmental Christians who are unbending sticklers concerning some aspect of Christianity; but, oddly, we give a pass to people who are extremists on the other end of the spectrum.

Some church-resistant people are sticklers about taking advantage of Biblical concepts that are not spelled out with the precision of a last will and testament or an international nuclear-arms treaty.

They do this not because they are endeavoring to uphold the integrity of the scripture but because they are looking for **loopholes**.

No, none of the inspired writers of the Bible recorded the exact words "Oh, ye people living from this date until the early 21st century and beyond, each and every one of you shall participate in a group meeting with other Christians, employing some sense of structure and pattern."

People who harp on these things like to think of themselves as Grammar Police or Political Fact-Checkers, but really and truly, they are **just trying to get away with something**.

Yes, Your Butt STILL BELONGS IN CHURCH

Such protestations are childish. And I'll give you an example, focusing on childish behavior.

Suppose a mother scolds her oldest son, "Be careful how you play! Don't hit your little brother with that hammer!"

Well, big brother scurries out to Dad's workshop, rifles through his father's toolbox until he finds another hammer, returns to the den, and proceeds to whack his younger sibling with the instrument.

This was not a misunderstanding. Big brother did not think that the second hammer would be any less painful than the first. He did not have any legitimate reason to interpret Mom's message as "I do want your precious little brother bashed, but with a different weapon." He just wanted to continue his horseplay, regardless of the danger posed to other family members. And he thought holding his mother to her exact words ("**that** hammer") would absolve him of any blame.

Most likely, the brat would earn himself an enthusiastic butt-whooping or (in a home opposed to corporal punishment) a month-long cessation of privileges.

In other words, trying to skirt through life via **technicalities** is fraught with consequences.

True, back in Genesis, in the days of the patriarchs, one seldom hears a discouraging word about a lone righteous person throwing together an altar made of stones and offering a sacrifice to the one genuine God.

But with the advent of the Law of Moses, things became more regimented. The Bible goes into excruciating detail about "thou shalts" and "thou shalt nots" and ceremonial washings and annual feast days and such.

Thankfully, the Christian dispensation is a whole lot more simplified, but it is still implicit that Christianity is

Yes, Your Butt STILL BELONGS IN CHURCH

something we practice not only when we're alone but in **groups** as well.

Jesus's followers were disillusioned when he was crucified, but after the resurrected Jesus made appearances over a 40-day period and ascended to heaven, they were emboldened. Acts 1:13-15 gives us an idea of their unity: "And when they were come in, they went up into an upper room, where abode both Peter, and James, and John, and Andrew, and Philip, and Thomas, Bartholomew, and Matthew, James, the son of Alphaeus, and Simon Zelotes, and Judas the brother of James. They all continued with one accord in prayer and supplication, with the women, and Mary the mother of Jesus, and with his brethren. And in those days Peter stood up in the midst of the disciples, and said (the number of names together were about an hundred and twenty) ..."

Acts 2:41-42 tells about the results of the apostles' historic sermon on the day of Pentecost: "Then they that gladly received his word were baptized: and the same day there were added unto them about three thousand souls. And they continued steadfastly in the apostles' doctrine and fellowship, and in breaking of bread, and in prayers."

Acts 2:46 tells about the converts exhibiting "gladness and singleness of heart." It's hard to have **singleness of heart** when some Christians are dutifully attending services (fellowship) and others are just "doing their own thang."

The remainder of Acts and the epistles are a history of churches being established and nourished. The evangelists yearned to visit or revisit the congregations – to settle a doctrinal dispute, to impart a spiritual gift, or to renew old acquaintances. Nowhere do they treat the churches as **unimportant**.

The book of Revelation minces no words in critiquing the "seven churches of Asia Minor." Some of the individual

Yes, Your Butt STILL BELONGS IN CHURCH

congregations are condemned for specific shortcomings such as complacency, but none are ridiculed for **existing**.

Nowhere in the Bible do we find God labeling those who faithfully serve him as overachievers, showoffs, worrywarts, or brown-nosers.

The Bible warns Christians to be vigilant about false teachers, heresies, apostasies, and schisms; but it does not tell us that being an active member of a congregation is optional or inadvisable.

It's just plain wrong to assert that congregations were a **necessary evil** in the first couple of centuries of the church (because of persecution, poverty, and the newness of the doctrine) but that we don't need them now.

Perhaps the church is **treated** as dispensable in the 21st century, but it has never been more indispensable.

Take an honest look at our society. There are phone apps for committing adultery. Looters are envious of what other people have earned. Sports gambling has been legalized. Conspicuous consumption has led to crushing credit card debt. A cult of self-worship exists. Pornography that once would have meant jail time is now readily available on our phones. Recreational use of marijuana keeps expanding. Abortion is treated as first-resort birth control method by many.

You can certainly address these issues all by yourself, but the pooled resources of the church remain the best way to shine light on the darkness of the world.

If you're going to play the nitpicking game and build your case on God not **mandating the details** of your modern-day church participation, two can play that game. I will point out that nowhere in scripture does God command, "Thou shalt write activities such as 'church,' 'yoga,' 'surfing,' 'flea-marketing,' 'deer-hunting,' 'skateboarding,'

Yes, Your Butt STILL BELONGS IN CHURCH

and 'chilling' on scraps of paper, put them in a bag, shake it up, and spend your time doing whatever word you pull out."

Humor me here. If we can agree that church attendance is not a **bad** thing, why can't you keep an open mind about its maybe being a **desirable** or **preferable** thing?

The only obstacle I see is a stiff-necked resistance to God's will.

Why reject a compliment from God? God has credited you with having enough **intelligence** to read between the lines and learn from the example of the early saints.

Use that intelligence. Don't try to prove God wrong.

Yes, Your Butt STILL BELONGS IN CHURCH

Excuse 38:
"Okay, okay -- I'll get around to church eventually"

Is your spiritual "plan of action" based on anecdotes about some 90-year-old "character" who used to live in your neighborhood?

It seems that a lot of never-Christians or lapsed Christians harbor a grudging admiration for a legendary codger who got to sow his wild oats **and** (just in the nick of time) "get right with the Lord."

This lovable reprobate spent decades cheating on his multiple wives, bombarding his poor liver with excessive amounts of alcohol, cussing like a sailor, and brawling with anyone who looked the wrong way at him.

Then, as he became frail and attended one too many funerals for his bosom pals, he decided to get baptized and hobble into the church building every time he was physically capable.

What a life! Satan **wants** us to think we can suck all the marrow out of life, run around without any rules, and then conveniently straighten things out at the last moment.

Yes, Your Butt STILL BELONGS IN CHURCH

The phrase "put your affairs in order" has become so ingrained in our minds that we assume that we will receive clear warning signs of when to begin the "tidying up" process.

Despite all evidence to the contrary, many of us carry with us the conceit that we will someday receive a terminal diagnosis ("I'm afraid you have only two years to live") and work on making amends at our own pace. We'll apologize to everyone we've wronged in our lives, put weeks of thought into a last will and testament, crack open our dust-encrusted Bible, and become Christians.

Alas, death does not always adhere to human timetables. "Healthy" people keel over with massive heart attacks. Gang violence claims innocent bystanders as well as gang members. Sleep-deprived medical professionals may accidentally turn a routine surgery into a fatal incident. Bald tires, rain-slicked roads, poorly maintained bridges, or downed electrical lines may kill young people who had dreamed of many years of great accomplishments ahead of them. Flash floods and forest fires don't care one whit what you had planned for next week.

We know the **perpetrators** of the 9-11 tragedy were on a suicide mission, but do you think any of the **victims** truly expected to die that particular day?

No matter how many preachers preach on the fragility of life or how many close friends warn of unsustainable lifestyles, some stubborn people keep kicking the can down the road.

They keep waiting for that white-coated doctor to give them a terminal diagnosis so they can make major changes in their life.

But…every human has **already** been given a terminal diagnosis.

Yes, Your Butt STILL BELONGS IN CHURCH

By the time you've flushed your first goldfish or been dragged along to some obscure great-uncle's funeral, you know that man is mortal and the clock is ticking.

By the time you understand right and wrong, you know you have an all-important choice to make.

Actually, there are **two** problems with a plan that consists of living like a heathen until you see those lab results and hear that prognosis from your doctor.

As I've written, there is absolutely no guarantee that your demise will be something you can **plan** for. Even responsible high school students can die because a stupid friend added something "funny" to the drinks or started brandishing an "unloaded" pistol. Young married couples die because they let the batteries in their smoke alarm expire. Middle-aged entrepreneurs on their way to receive an award die because of a faulty automotive airbag.

Second, even if your death is **not** sudden, the longer you stay away from Christ and the church, the more hardened your heart becomes. You may **tell** yourself that you will spring into action once the diagnosis of cancer or kidney failure is presented, but there is a strong possibility you **won't**. Whether you are given six weeks or six months or six years, when you draw your last breath, you may be no closer to serving God than when you were healthy and carefree.

Salesmen tell us there is no time like **now** to teach your toddlers French or start a college savings program for them. Salesmen tell us there is no time like **now** to lock in insurance rates or mortgage rates. Salesmen tell us there is no time like **now** to inspect and repair your home, staying one step ahead of problems that will assuredly become more costly as the years go by.

Yes, Your Butt STILL BELONGS IN CHURCH

Well, there is no time like **now** to dedicate your life to Christ.

If that message doesn't sink in immediately, I hope you will reread this tomorrow.

But I can't guarantee you'll be more open-minded -- or even **alive** -- then.

No one can.

Section 3

All out of excuses; now what?

What concerned Christians can do

What can one lone Christian do to promote the survival and future of the church?

More than you might realize.

In Christianity as in breadmaking, "A little leaven leaveneth the whole lump" (Galatians 5:9). You can have a tremendous positive (or negative) influence on your family, the family in the next pew, visitors to the church, and your friends.

Try to be a **well-balanced Christian**. The cause of Christ is held back by those who are Christian In Name Only as well as those who are obnoxiously super-religious.

(Remember, there are widows who take care of stray animals, and then there are "crazy cat ladies." There are people who show the love of Jesus in their lives, and then there are "religious nuts.")

Set a good example for your spouse, children, and grandchildren. Don't treat Sunday morning church attendance as a chore. Be regular and on time. Show up in time for Bible study, not just the part where the preacher does all the heavy lifting. Pay attention to the sermon (the preacher could be saying something that will change your outlook on the week **or** he could be saying something

Yes, Your Butt STILL BELONGS IN CHURCH

unscriptural that needs to be addressed) instead of daydreaming about lunch or the afternoon's football game.

Take the time to greet visitors. Don't assume it's "somebody else's job" to make them feel welcome. Read the body language of visitors; let them know you care, without coming across as nosey and prying.

Don't burn rubber getting out of the parking lot. Stay for some Christian fellowship. After you **are** away from the church grounds, don't spend the time gossiping about how much weight someone has put on or whining about how lousy the sermon was.

Even if you're only one person among 20 or among 500 or among 5,000, express your concerns. If there is something your congregation is doing wrong or something they're doing that is good but could be even better, let your opinions be known.

Pray even when you're not in church. Pray when you arise, when you eat, when you go to bed. Not just cookie-cutter perfunctory prayers, but specific, heartfelt prayers. Pray in times of personal or national crisis (and triumph). Don't make prayer a last resort.

Study your Bible even if it's not Sunday. It's admirable to pass the time learning a new language or reading up on how to perform routine home repairs, but nothing is more important than regular Bible study.

Find teachable moments for your family. But don't become a caricature like Ned Flanders on *The Simpsons*. It is possible to have an underlying appreciation of God's gifts without greeting every mundane occurrence with "Praise God! I found a penny!" or "Thank you, Jesus, for not letting me walk into that spider web!" Such outbursts can turn people off.

Yes, Your Butt STILL BELONGS IN CHURCH

Make "extracurricular" church events **available** to your children and grandchildren, but don't **overbook** them on church camp and the like. That's a good way to produce burnout.

When your children fly the nest (going off to college, moving for a job, starting their own family) and pop in for weekend visits, in a loving, non-judgmental way let them know that you plan to be in church and that people would love to see them. Their presence at church may not be "fun," but it's more rewarding than just hanging out with their old high school friends at the diner.

The workplace is another location for taking a balanced approach to Christianity. You need to be somewhere **between** secretive and "in your face" about your walk with Christ.

If your workspace is festooned with inspirational quotes, crucifixes, Jesus pictures, and tons of other physical manifestations of your inner self, it will be hard for people to view you as an approachable, three-dimensional human being. On the other hand, if you quietly read the Bible during breaktime, you may start some conversations.

Don't make co-workers hide from you on Monday morning because they know you'll dominate the conversation with breathless details of the church service. On the other hand, don't be **ashamed** of your Christianity; if someone asks, "What did you do over the weekend?," you can give a concise, nonjudgmental account of your worship instead of a demure "Oh, nothing much."

If you decide that you have been a lackluster (or downright offensive) Christian, don't beat yourself up. Make amends and redouble your efforts to do better in the future.

Or if you feel that you've worked hard for Jesus but not seen any visible results (your children have stopped attending, none of the friends have accepted your invitations, etc.), again, don't beat yourself up. Be patient. You'll have your reward, and God may surprise you with changes in the attitude of others. You won't be able to help **anyone** if you give up in despair.

Finally, make use of those apologetics books mentioned in an earlier chapter. You don't have to toss out crime novels or romance novels or outdoors magazines, but apologetics books are more substantive in the long run. They can uplift you, fortify your faith, and help you make the case for Christ in a more articulate manner.

What church leaders can do

My next book will probably be about marriage. In fact, I finished the manuscript nearly **five years ago**; but my wife wanted me to do further editing ("Leave out that personal stuff!"), so the project wound up on the back burner.

One of the opening chapters of that so-far-unpublished book deals with **finding** a good person to date and marry.

I start out by asking, "What makes you think you **deserve** a good mate?"

I then go through all sorts of quirks, prejudices, baggage, and character flaws that could seriously narrow the number of people who would want to be seen in your company, let alone make a **lifelong commitment** to you.

I think a similar situation applies to the church.

Church leaders (elders, deacons, ministers, etc.), what exactly makes you think your congregation, your denomination, or even Christendom as a whole **deserves** to survive and grow?

Are you teaching the same message that the church's founder (Jesus Christ) taught, or have you let all sorts of man-made theories, regulations, and workarounds creep in?

Yes, Your Butt STILL BELONGS IN CHURCH

(I know it's a scary prospect to question everything you've ever been taught; but in the mission fields, entire congregations may decide that they are in error and switch their affiliation.)

Do you have the love and zeal of Jesus in your heart, or is your place of worship just another **social club**?

In a modern world with innumerable ways to spend a Sunday morning and innumerable alleged "paths to enlightenment," what makes what you are offering unique, irreplaceable, and life-affirming?

No, don't just plow through to the end of the chapter. Lay this book aside. **Examine** the structure of the early church and compare it with what you have. **Ponder** the enthusiasm of the early converts. Discuss among yourselves the doctrinal disputes and compromises that have arisen in the evolution of how you worship now.

If you can search your heart and declare, "Yes, we **deserve** to survive and grow," read on.

Before we even get to the doctrinal message, certainly, **amenities** are important.

Your church building doesn't have to be ostentatious (the first-century meeting places certainly weren't), but to be appealing to visitors it needs to have a clean, well-kept exterior, adequate parking, good acoustics (e.g. not a loudspeaker that sounds like the devil's fiddle playing in *The Devil Went Down To Georgia*), good lighting, good air conditioning, good plumbing (our church building had only an outhouse until I was in my teens, a situation that would give a lot of people an excuse not to attend nowadays), and adequate supplies for the classrooms.

Different congregations have different budgets, but do the best with what you have to make the place presentable and physically comfortable.

Yes, Your Butt STILL BELONGS IN CHURCH

Signage and marketing can help the church stay visible. If you have a billboard with a pithy inspirational quote, don't leave the message unchanged or missing letters for weeks on end; that demonstrates that no one really cares.

Some newspapers place ads in the newspaper. Some get the newspaper to print sermonettes by the preacher. If you're not already doing this, consider it.

Many churches have church bulletins, but these periodicals can take on the stink of **junk mail**. They shouldn't be drudge work; take some **pride** in them. There will **always** be a percentage of members who pass up the chance to read the prayer lists and events schedules; but settling for unattractive typography and graphics will only make it **easier** for them to ignore the newsletter. Maybe dear old Mabel, who has been typing up the bulletin since Eisenhower was president, needs some tips and assistance for sprucing up the bulletin.

15-minute sermons have been a staple of my local radio station for decades. Some churches can afford TV broadcasts. I have also seen churches run professionally produced ads along with movie trailers in the theater.

Social media may be ubiquitous, but they are underused for Jesus. People tend to think that if the congregation itself has a website or Facebook page, that's good enough. Individual members need to be encouraged to share their Christian witness through their **personal** social media posts. Don't hide your light under a basket!

See that everyone in the congregation has something to do – either in public worship or in support services. If you keep piling all the responsibilities on the same handful of workhorses, you will miss out on hidden talents **and** work the workhorses to death (or at least until they burn out).

Yes, Your Butt STILL BELONGS IN CHURCH

Keep a good working relationship with neighboring congregations, so you can share resources, opportunities, and warnings (con men preying upon churches, etc.)

Old-fashioned potluck "dinner-on-the-grounds" events attract more alumni than unchurched guests, but they **can** keep the church visible, nonetheless.

Be transparent about your finances. If you're sitting on a pile of money, some congregation member might know a great way to use it in the service of the Lord. If you're barely scraping by, members need to be aware of it so they can suggest remedies. Secrecy breeds distrust in any organization.

Do some community surveys; then have brainstorming sessions to address ways in which the church is falling short. For instance, I don't agree 100 percent with the contents of David Murrow's book *Why Men Hate Going to Church*, but Murrow has valid points about reasons the stereotypical "man's man" feels conspicuous in a traditional church setting. I would recommend perusing the book and debating its suggestions.

As resources permit, do some outreach work in the community: knocking on doors, hosting informational kiosks at craft fairs, sponsoring English as Second Language classes, conducting grief counseling sessions, etc.

Some churches place a special emphasis on **branding.** Perhaps they want to be seen as a casual, laid-back, jeans-and-sneakers sort of church. Or they want to specialize in helping unwed mothers. That's fine, as long as you don't drive anyone **away.** One congregation in Minnesota got a lot of blowback when it tried to adopt a more youthful appeal and encouraged its current members to go somewhere else (!) for a couple of years!

Yes, Your Butt STILL BELONGS IN CHURCH

Do an honest assessment of your **hospitality**. Even if you have ushers with the **job** of greeting and seating visitors, it makes a bad impression on visitors when the regular membership ignores them.

Watch out for cliques. It's natural that members who have something else in common besides their Christianity (live on the same street, went to the same school, have kids the same age, etc.) will chat more before and after services, but it's important that everyone feels like one big family.

This is a tricky issue, but practice some **quality control** of preachers and teachers. Don't **spy** on the kiddie classes, but sit in on a class occasionally to make sure the teacher isn't in over his/her head. If the preacher is constantly pontificating on weighty matters that sail over the head of 75 percent of the congregation, maybe you have a bad fit. If the preacher never quotes scripture, harps on the same subject every week, or puts everyone to sleep, you have a problem – a problem that needs to be handled in a **diplomatic manner**.

It's a daunting task, but it's worthwhile to take special care with touchy subjects. Preachers and teachers don't have to walk on eggshells, but neither should they be **tone deaf**. It is easy to blurt out something that will offend unwed mothers, divorcees, converts from other denominations, former inmates, members who can't get their spouse to attend, and other groups. There are hard truths that all of us need to hear, but sometimes we can be unforgivably blunt and thoughtless in our comments.

A robust teenager class is vital. I cringe to think of this critical age group (will they abandon church at age 18 or serve Christ for the rest of their lives?) being in the hands of a 40-year-old nerd who is unsuccessfully trying to be cool. Your youth program doesn't have to **condone** everything going on in popular culture, but it needs to be **aware** of personalities and trends. The teachers need to

Yes, Your Butt STILL BELONGS IN CHURCH

remember what it was like to be an awkward, hormonal teenager. And they need to be willing and able to discuss relevant topics such as bisexuality, drug abuse, and revolving-door stepparents.

Follow up with transplants and new converts. "Babes in Christ" need a lot of guidance. One member of my congregation satirized a prevalent attitude as "Ha ha! We've got him in the club now! Now we can take him for granted!"

Heartfelt shouts of "Amen!" make one stand out like a sore thumb in many modern churches, and mainstream churches have never really caught on to the "call and response" pattern of black spirituals; but services do need to be interactive and demand something of the pew-occupiers.

Prayers should be fresh and earnest, not paint-by-numbers enterprises. It's good for the song leader to bring up fond memories or background information of the hymns on his list. Adult Bible classes are not designed for a **lecturer**; there should be lots of give and take. The communion service is not a time for daydreaming or balancing your check book. In recent times, some of the people conducting our communion service, rather than muttering the same old phrases, have made a **point** of metaphorically whacking people over the head with a two-by-four -- spotlighting the solemnity and symbolism of the ritual.

But don't ever get **desperate** enough to bend or water down your doctrine just to get people through the door. It may make you feel good in the short run, but it is akin to negotiating with hostage takers and is a recipe for an eventual death spiral.

And don't let the **quest for numbers** tempt you to pander to thrill seekers. We are blessed to have tools for keeping up with today's shortened attention spans, but at

Yes, Your Butt STILL BELONGS IN CHURCH

some point, the pyrotechnics and showmanship seem to become more important than the core message.

You may see short-term gains, but you will **never** be able to compete with the world for **adrenaline junkies**. Legalized marijuana is big business in the U.S.; but bootleg marijuana remains popular, because people want something **stronger**. And your superficial converts will eventually decide, "Hey, why should I go to **church** for a rock concert when I can go to a **real** rock concert **and** get sex???"

Finally, start and maintain a church library of apologetics literature. Pique the curiosity of members by announcing the latest addition. The church cannot prosper if the preacher and teachers are the only ones who are expected to know the Bible.

What those outside the church can do

I can still remember the first time I saw the Village People perform their iconic hit *Y.M.C.A.*

I was at college in the fall of 1978 and they appeared on the short-lived NBC variety show *Dick Clark's Live Wednesday*.

To this day, the line that (well, for lack of a better word) **resonates** with me is "Young man, young man, put your pride on the shelf."

Whether you are man or woman, young or old, faithful Christian or outsider, it pays to have some **humility** when grappling with questions of spirituality.

If you have resisted attending church regularly, returning to church, or learning more about church, you need to do a painfully honest assessment of your motivations.

All those times you were snubbed or disrespected in church...were those **objective events** or were they matters of your perceptions and preconceptions?

Did you honestly try to fit in, participate, study? Did you ask questions so you could learn, or just to be a class clown?

Yes, Your Butt STILL BELONGS IN CHURCH

Is the church building the only place you display attention deficit disorder, or is it something that plagues you in life in general?

If you can honestly say that you were done wrong by fellow Christians or let down by the preacher, and no one is willing to make amends, that's one thing. But ask yourself if it's fair to extrapolate and blame every clergyman, every usher, every choir director, every church bus driver **worldwide** for those shortcomings.

If you're a reasonable person, you'll realize that you need to find a more suitable church home instead of going **cold turkey** on Christianity.

What about your support system? Are you the only person in your social circle of friends who harbors such disdain for church, or are they **reinforcing** your attitudes?

Do your friends make you a better or worse person?

Are they a true sounding board, busting your chops when you espouse something stupid, or are they just an echo chamber, a rubber stamp, a gaggle of "yes men"?

Do they have your best interests at heart, or are they just fair-weather friends? (A good indicator is the ratio of "Thanks for visiting my nana in the hospital" to "Wasn't that an awesome pub crawl?" messages in your texts and social media postings.)

Sometimes when your friends are messing up your romance or putting you in danger of being fired from your job, you must level with them or reduce your exposure to them. If they're keeping you away from **church**, the stakes are even higher.

Surely, you've wronged or disappointed someone in your life and been granted a second chance? Why not give a second chance to public worship?

Yes, Your Butt STILL BELONGS IN CHURCH

Society places great emphasis on walking a mile in someone else's moccasins. Apply that to faithful Christians. It's easy for nonbelievers to adopt a Tom Petty attitude of "You don't know how it feels to be me," but it's hypocritical not to extend the same deference to Christians.

Don't just hate, mock, or pity Christians. Try to understand **why** Jesus and public worship are so important to their lives.

Finally, just like practicing Christians, you need to avail yourself of some apologetics books.

Whether you you're leery of church because you believe quantum physics could just create the universe out of nothing or because you feel the Bible has been mistranslated beyond recognition over the years or because you think the Bible contradicts itself, you can find guidance and answers in apologetics books.

I can't force you to read them, but you know it's the **right thing to do**. Whether you're trying to land a job, make a good impression on a date, flip a house, or win a government grant, it's vital to **avail yourself of all the pertinent information**.

Maybe you just don't like reading. Maybe you're afraid of what you might find ("My engine is not making a funny sound, my engine is not making a funny sound, my engine is not making a funny sound..."). But it is vitally important that you get the full picture of what God and Christ have in store for you.

Maybe you are plagued by doubts now, but if you are diligent enough, some day you will develop confidence. You will be able to apply the instructions of Hebrews 4:16: "Let us therefore come boldly unto the throne of grace, that we may obtain mercy, and find grace to help in time of need."

A final plea for apologetics

By now you probably think I'm flogging a dead horse about apologetics but hear me out.

I must keep pounding the idea home because so many Christians treat "apologetics" as a dirty word from the get-go.

They think that augmenting the bare-bones Bible with anything else is a display of weakness and lack of faith.

Using apologetics is a recognition that God has blessed us with Christian thinkers who can **bring order out of chaos** when dealing with the public's misperceptions.

There's an old saying: "It's a poor workman who blames his tools." What kind of workman are you if you won't even **try using** your tools?

God has inspired Christians with the research skills and writing skills to make the Bible more understandable, but many people have a vampire-seeing-a-crucifix reaction to apologetics.

"Give me that old-time religion, it's good enough for me" is the mantra of many Christians. They are probably harking back to the two decades after World War II, when church membership was booming; but the **truly** old-time religion was powered by the fact that **eyewitnesses** of Jesus could

Yes, Your Butt STILL BELONGS IN CHURCH

go out and convince their friends of his divinity and his plan of salvation. We no longer have eyewitnesses, but we do have **authors** who can show why the **accounts** of the eyewitnesses are still credible today.

In your daily life of dealing with family members, co-workers, and neighbors, how much respect have you really won by repeating the same thing only **louder**? How many foreigners have you given clear instructions by saying the same word over and over, louder each time?

God wants the church populated with human beings, not with **parrots**. ("Awk! Polly wants a communion wafer!") Merely regurgitating verses that you don't really understand is not a good plan.

Do you truly think you can glide through life with the same lack of preparation that many people have for religion?

If a student is given an essay assignment such as "Why my dad is the greatest dad in the world" or "Why my dog is the greatest dog in the world," they **could** scribble down "Duh. They just **are**. This is a dumb assignment." The student would probably receive a failing grade.

If a job interviewer asks an applicant, "Why makes you think you're a good fit for this company?" and he snaps back, "I don't know. I just **am**. Say, how many absences is a new employee allowed?" he will probably not get the job.

If your Significant Other is feeling down in the dumps, they may start fishing for compliments. If they ask, "Why do you love me?" an answer of "I don't know. I just do. What's for supper?" will not promote peace and harmony in the household.

I accept that Jesus is the Son of God and offers salvation. **I** accept that the Bible is the inspired word of God. Maybe you do, too. But that's just half our obligation. We must also care enough to develop the **reasoning skills** and **people skills** necessary to **share** the message.

The Bible tells us that it is the Word of God, transcribed by holy men working under the inspiration of the Holy Spirit. Bless the Christians who accept that without argument. But it's understandable that some people will balk. **Lots** of religious texts claim to be "the answer," just as countless secular books (by their title or their marketing campaign) make audacious claims about how authoritative they are. Think *The Last Book About Ferret Farming You'll Ever Need* or *The Ultimate Guide to Lawnmower Gaskets* or *The Never-Fail Guide to Meeting Women*.

Given all the hucksters and charlatans in the world, it is entirely reasonable for someone to ask, "Okay, what are your **credentials** for writing about ferret farming?" or "How do you **know** the Bible is any more true than these other sacred texts?"

Whether you're talking about a secular book or the Bible, a round of hemming and hawing, sputtering, and yelling, "You're just too dumb to understand, you heathen!" is not going to close the deal. The more flustered a Christian becomes, the more ammunition he gives to Satan.

The attitude of Never-Apologetics Christians is hypocritical. When they make decisions in their everyday lives, they want to read book reviews and Yelp reviews and ask probing questions of an acquaintance who is raving about a new restaurant. But when they promote Christianity, they suddenly take an approach of "It's my way or the highway!"

Not everyone is nimble on their feet when encountering questions out of left field, but many "devout" Christians cannot counter even the most **predictable** objections from skeptics.

Yes, Your Butt STILL BELONGS IN CHURCH

When a young person raised in the church starts expressing doubts, or when a non-Christian at work starts asking tentative questions, we should be able to sit down with them and say, "I can understand why these conflicting genealogies or census results disturb you. Let me show you how they really **don't** contradict one another."

When an unbeliever comes at you with a "Gotcha!" question about some mythical tribe mentioned in the Bible, you should be able to say, "Yes, for centuries Bible critics claimed that those people were just made up by a fanciful Bible author, but in 1975 archaeologists found abundant evidence that the civilization actually did exist, just like the Bible said."

Yes, you can cobble together some sort of presentation based strictly on the Bible, but as one writer pointed out, apologetics let you give a more **robust** response to naysayers.

Yes, you will have to sort through apologetics books based on your reading skills and whether you want a broad "cheat sheet" version or something focused on a particular issue, such as "Does science contradict the Bible?"

But the sorting process is well worth the effort. (And no one requires you to stop at **one** book.)

Do you want it on your conscience that someone is left out of the Lamb's Book of Life because **you** were too proud or too stubborn to crack open an apologetics book?

Yes, Your Butt **STILL BELONGS IN CHURCH**

Why has this book taken so long?

As we approach the final chapter, some of you may be thinking, "If this topic of church attendance is so urgent, and if the replies to the excuses are so blindingly obvious to you, what took you so long to publish this book?"

Well, besides the myriad interruptions of daily life, **this chapter** has taken up an inordinate amount of time. I have proceeded cautiously with it because of a line from the Hippocratic Oath: "First, do no harm."

Words have meanings. Words sometimes need warning labels. Words sometimes have unintended consequences.

No, I'm not trying to make this like a cheesy ad for a mail-order martial arts manual. ("You must take a blood oath not to use the forbidden secrets in this book to kick your fellow sixth-graders through a brick wall.")

I just want to proceed deliberately and anticipate misguided takeaways.

Where lapsed Christians are concerned, when it comes to doling out advice, I don't want to be regarded as "that guy."

I don't want to be that guy – the clueless do-gooder (with no skin in the game) who blithely tells a stranger to get right back on the horse that threw him. I don't want to be the sanctimonious twit who tells a spousal abuse victim,

Yes, Your Butt STILL BELONGS IN CHURCH

"It's your duty to go right back into your home and act as if nothing happened." Those people tend to act like **innocent bystanders** if someone gets **beaten to death**.

Speaking as someone who doesn't know the particulars of your case, I want to be measured in my advice. If you think your misgivings about the church can be worked out in an amicable manner, go for it.

On the other hand, if you have truly been treated in an unchristian manner, if you witness corruption and sin going unaddressed, if the people you've placed your faith in can't answer even the most basic questions...I'm **not** going to insist that you march back into the same church building, plop down on the same pew, and deliver an Oliver Twist-like "Please, sir...I want some **more**."

There are good individual Christians out there. There are good congregations out there. Just as you keep looking for the right doctor or the right repairman, you need to keep looking until you find the right spiritual community.

I don't want to give the impression that it's as simple as picking the first name that comes up on a Google search of "churches in my area" and making a lifetime commitment to that group.

Finding a church that is **pleasing to God** (and not just to you) takes a lot of thought, research, and prayer.

But, as the saying goes, anything worth doing is worth doing well.

Where generic church leaders are concerned, I don't want them to take it for granted that they have me solidly in their corner. I don't feel I have an obligation to give a **blanket endorsement** to anything and everything that slaps the word "church" over its front door.

Yes, Your Butt STILL BELONGS IN CHURCH

This would be like advising someone, "Well, those blood pressure pills look sort of like the ones I take, so I'm sure they're okay for you" or "I've never eaten at that restaurant, but the sign says 'Gourmet dining,' so it has to be good."

Let's face it: Christianity has become a hot mess.

God told Noah and his family, "Be ye fruitful and multiply"; but nowhere did He say the same thing about producing hundreds and thousands of different **denominations**. Nowhere did God describe the church as a giddily creative Build-A-Bear workshop.

And this confusion may be doing Christianity **more damage than all the other excuses rolled together**.

I know it's a big "if," but **if** the church had delivered a unified (Godly) message over the past two millennia (instead of members getting their panties in a wad over a single obscure verse or questing for the newest flavor of spirituality), there would be fewer empty pews and immeasurably less human suffering.

The "big tent" picture of spirituality ("Everybody's going to heaven, they're just taking different roads") is not only unscriptural, but also **demonstrably full of hooey**.

Don't pretend that all churches are the same.

Some churches teach that God created the universe and then split for parts unknown; others feel that He takes an active role in human history and answers our prayers.

Some churches teach that Jesus is the Son part of the Trinity; others teach that the Trinity is a false concept.

Some churches teach that Satan is a fallen angel, the tempter who corrupts mankind; others teach that he is just a metaphor.

Yes, Your Butt STILL BELONGS IN CHURCH

Some churches teach that Adam and Noah and those other chaps from the early chapters of Genesis are actual historical figures; other churches say they are just folklore.

Some churches teach that hell means eternal punishment; some teach that it is a merciful instant annihilation; others teach that it's just an idea.

Some churches teach that an individual's salvation or condemnation is **predestined**; others teach that our fate is changeable.

Some churches teach that baptism (by immersion) is necessary for salvation; others teach that baptism is just an extra sign and can take several forms.

Some churches allow female clergy; others forbid it.

Some churches perform gay and lesbian weddings; others would die first.

Some churches dutifully carry out a communion service each week; others observe it monthly or quarterly.

Some churches insist on a literal Six Days of Creation; some are more accommodating to the billions of years accepted by most scientists.

Some (most) churches teach that Sunday is the day for public worship; others insist that Saturday is the true day of worship.

Some churches freely associate and cooperate with other denominations; others would consider this to be giving aid and comfort to the enemy.

Some churches teach that the Rapture and Tribulation as seen in apocalyptic literature are actual discernible events; other churches see them as symbolic.

Yes, Your Butt STILL BELONGS IN CHURCH

Some churches teach tithing (giving 10 percent of one's earthly gain) as a hard and fast, enforced-by-the-church mandate; others leave giving up to the conscience of the individual.

Some churches believe in getting militantly involved with "Social Justice Warrior"-type causes; others strive to keep religion and politics separate.

Some churches teach that each congregation should be independent and self-governing; others teach that a strong centralized governing body is necessary.

Some churches teach that miraculous gifts (speaking in tongues, prophesying, healing) are still in effect; other churches feel that such manifestations of the Holy Spirit faded away after the Bible was compiled.

Some churches teach that the Bible is sufficient; others teach that we need a ton of additional creeds, catechisms, observances, feasts, prohibitions, etc.

Some churches are "all fire and brimstone, all the time"; others emphasize the touchy-feely, "I'm okay, you're okay" aspects of religion.

Some churches shame and excommunicate members right and left; others never discipline anyone for **anything**.

True, on some nonessential matters, churches can safely agree to disagree. But churches also contradict one another on issues that are vital and **nonnegotiable**. Jesus either is or **isn't** the Son of God. Either hell exists or it **doesn't** exist. Prayers are answered or they **aren't** answered.

Not all the organizations identifying as churches can be right. They simply can't.

And people seeking an excuse for not being a Christian seize solace in the 1967 Buffalo Springfield song *For What*

Yes, Your Butt STILL BELONGS IN CHURCH

It's Worth ("There's battle lines being drawn/And nobody's right if everybody's wrong.")

But the mere existence of competing claims doesn't necessarily prove that **no one** can be right.

Every convenience market in a municipality may brag "Coldest beer in town," but that doesn't prove they're **all** wrong. If you take your trusty thermometer from store to store, you will eventually discover the market that has the chilliest brew.

Yes, this means a lot of legwork; but if you're truly a connoisseur of cold beer, you will make the effort. Just as you would make the effort to find the right accountant, piano teacher, automotive mechanic...or path to God.

By way of full disclosure, I consider myself to be a plain Christian. For the past six decades, I have found well-thought-out comfort in a building with the designation "Church of Christ" (not to be confused with either the Church of Jesus Christ of Latter Day Saints or the Disciples of Christ).

I have never seen a **perfect** group of people worshipping under the name Church of Christ, but most of us are trying. The Church of Christ grew out of the Restoration Movement of the early 19th century. (Wikipedia describes the Restoration Movement as "a converging of Christians across denominational lines in search of a return to an original, 'pre-denominational' Christianity.")

The unofficial motto is "Speak where the Bible speaks and remain silent where the Bible is silent."

I have been able to feel **safe** but not **complacent** in this environment. There is plenty of room to assess my personal shortcomings (especially sins of omission), but I do not feel compelled to jump out of bed every morning rubbing my hands together and scheming, "Now, what can

Yes, Your Butt STILL BELONGS IN CHURCH

I rationalize, dismiss, mold to fit 21st-century sensibilities, or take out of context **today**?"

Perhaps you've heard of Churches of Christ through the TV show *Duck Dynasty*. Both Phil Robertson and his son Alan are elders at White's Ferry Church of Christ in West Monroe, Louisiana.

Do a simple Google search and you'll find several references to "Why I am a member of the Church of Christ," for instance, this link to a PDF file: http://summitchurchofchrist.com/wp-content/uploads/2017/09/Topical-Study_Why-I-Am-a-Member-of-the-Church-of-Christ.pdf

"Aha!" some of you may shout. "Now the truth comes out! I thought this was going to be a useful book, but Tyree waited until the next to last chapter to reveal that it's all just a **bait-and-switch** scam! The whole book is a **Trojan horse** for Church of Christ propaganda!"

Wrong.

I'm not going to hand you a list that decrees, "You cannot deviate more than five percent from the way Tyree worships." I'm not going to declare that you're going to hell if you don't have a particular name on your church stationery. I'm not going to check up on you and judge you.

I may be the most **subversive** conservative Christian you ever encounter. I just want you to **think** about what you're doing or not doing.

Call it covering my own butt if you wish; but for my own peace of mind and clear conscience, I want to stress that Christianity is not something to be entered (or reentered) **lightly**.

Yes, Your Butt STILL BELONGS IN CHURCH

It's like a pharmacist reciting the side effects of a medicine, or a gun dealer running a background check. People have no control over how you use/abuse a pill, a firearm, or a book; but they're obligated to make you **think** about the gravity of what you're doing.

Here come the music lyrics again. Like the 1964 song recorded by Nina Simone, The Animals, and other artists, "I'm just a soul whose intentions are good/Oh Lord, please don't let me be misunderstood."

I want to inspire you, but I don't want the takeaway of this book to be "Any port in a storm." I refuse to place my stamp of approval on **anything and everything** that self-identifies as Christian.

We can always use more people who declare Jesus Christ as the Son of God and try to live a moral life, but there's more to it than that.

Meekly, cautiously, prayerfully striving to articulate this disclaimer is what has slowed me down in getting this book completed, but I couldn't sleep soundly at night unless I did my due diligence.

In 2 John 1:9-11, John warns, "Whosoever transgresseth and abideth not in the doctrine of Christ, hath not God. He that abideth in the doctrine of Christ, he hath both the Father and the Son. If there come any unto you, and bring not this doctrine, receive him not into your house, neither bid him God speed: For he that biddeth him God speed is partaker of his evil deeds."

That scripture is always in the back of my mind if someone hands me a pamphlet with ideas that are 180 degrees different from my understanding of the Bible. I'm courteous, but I can't bring myself to gladhand them and gush, "Well, that ain't my cup'a tea, man, but maybe you'll have better luck next door. Good luck."

Yes, Your Butt STILL BELONGS IN CHURCH

I have struggled with my misgivings about the potential misuse of this book; but after fervent prayers, I have decided that this book has the potential to **do more good than harm** for the cause of Christ, else I would not be wasting my time on it.

But the mitigation of harm requires communicating the seriousness of my concerns. This is not a "Be sure to gamble responsibly" addendum to a lottery commercial. I am **not** saying, "Take what you've learned in this book and (wink wink) use it properly."

I am imploring you to make wise choices with the ideas I have shared.

Parting Words

Thank you for putting up with this nearly novel-length treatise.

I'm sure there are wordsmiths who could have been much more eloquent in getting these sentiments across; but, then, it doesn't take a Shakespeare to yell, "Watch out for that car!" or a Steinbeck to whisper, "I think that creep slipped a date-rape drug into your punch."

Sometimes you just need somebody **competent** to get an urgent warning out there!

And I can't think of any warning that is more urgent than the one I have tried to announce in my own ham-handed manner. People are currently obsessed with being on "the right side of history," but what's truly important is being on the right side of **eternity**.

I am not in the market for hate mail, but constructive criticism is always welcome. I do hope you will let me know if I haven't been quite persuasive enough with some of my arguments or if you have encountered excuses that were not covered in my list.

I feel relieved to be typing the last few paragraphs of this manuscript, but *Yes, Your Butt Still Belongs in Church* will always be a **work in progress**. Thanks to the wonders of Kindle Direct Publishing and its print-on-demand service, I can make minor or major changes to future editions in a matter of minutes.

Yes, Your Butt STILL BELONGS IN CHURCH

Regardless of how many times I revise this book, I realize it is not a magic bullet. Some people will oppose the truth no matter what you say. But if we can lead even one person to Christ (or back to Christ), all my typing will have been worth it.

Once my fingerprints grow back, I hope to revamp my marriage book, pick up again with my sanctity-of-life book, and initiate some other projects; but my writing is a sideline, so I'm counting on you to make **this** book a success, which will give me more breathing space for subsequent projects.

I'm doing my best to convince people of the vanity and disastrous consequences of their excuse-making. And when I feel inadequate, I remember the words my father said his high school teacher Mr. Seay spoke nearly 80 years ago. A frustrated student declared that he had done his best on a problem. Mr. Seay reassured him, "Even the angels in heaven **can't do any better than their best**."

I may eventually schedule some book signings or lectures; but even if I do, I know I'll never meet most of you in the flesh. But let's **do our best** to see that someday a great gathering of us (and generations yet unborn) can enjoy fellowship in an upper and better kingdom.

May God bless.

Made in the USA
Columbia, SC
22 November 2020